BRITISH HISTORY

In brief

*A whistle-stop tour through
the history of Britain*

RALPH INGHAM-JOHNSON

First published in Great Britain as a softback original in 2020

Copyright © Ralph Ingham-Johnson

The moral right of this author has been asserted.

Typeset in Averia Serif Libre

Editing, design, typesetting and publishing by UK Book Publishing

www.ukbookpublishing.com

ISBN: 978-1-913179-57-1

To *Elouise*, my beloved wife, for her
encouragement and forbearance.

To *Elouise*, my beloved wife, for her encouragement and forbearance.

Contents

Foreword

This book is intended, primarily, for those who want a short overview of British history and an easy reference as to when and where and why incidents of importance took place, and if there is anything of interest to be seen there. For that reason, those occasions are described and, where possible, locations are given. Many of the references are made deliberately because they relate to ancient monuments which tourists might visit. This is not for a serious student of British history, who is better served by the work of the many distinguished historians and archaeologists, of whom some are mentioned later.

In some ways, Britain tends to be rather casual about its history. Whilst we are diligent in the preservation of historic buildings and other artefacts, ancient houses are still lived in as private houses and historic inns are likely to be exactly that. The famous Arlington Row cottages at Bibury in the Cotswolds are a typical example: built in the late 14th century, nevertheless, they are still lived in – and even today, you can walk in to an ancient tavern or historic inn and buy a pint of ale. In central London, for example, there are public houses which, a few hundred years ago, served food and drink to Samuel Pepys; the visitor can eat and drink in those very rooms. Britain has thousands of such premises up and down the country. Historic buildings that are open to the public, apart from churches, tend to have been the houses of important historic figures or castles and are usually treated as museums.

The Geography of Britain

The mainland of Great Britain is some 800 miles (1300Km) north to south and 450 miles (725Km) east to west. The east and south of the country are lowland areas and the west and north west are regarded as upland areas. Mountains in Britain are not high by European standards, the highest being Ben Nevis in Scotland, which is 4406 feet (1343m) high, with a reasonable path to the summit. Visitors from mainland Europe should be aware that this modest height notwithstanding, the weather in our upland and mountain areas is far from trustworthy and cannot safely be visited in light summer clothes as is normal in alpine and other mountain ranges in Europe. The weather can change from one extreme to the other in a very short space of time. The reason for this is that our upland areas are exposed to the North Atlantic, with only a little shelter from Ireland.

England has several upland areas, the largest being the Pennine Chain, which runs from Derby in the Midlands northward along the centre of the country to the Scottish border. The south-west of the country has two upland areas in Devon, Dartmoor and Exmoor and another in Cornwall. Further east are the gentler and climatically more moderate areas of the Cotswold Hills and the Chiltern Hills.

Further north, we have the Lake District, which is the wettest part of the country and one of the most beautiful. The lakes themselves are well developed to welcome tourists but the fells and mountains themselves are best left to those with mountaineering skills and equipment.

South Wales has the Brecon Beacons, which can be very hot in summer but very cold in winter. The middle of Wales is thinly populated moorland and the north is mountainous, culminating in the Snowdonia area which has extensive areas over 3000ft (920m). When rain falls in Snowdonia, it often has a brisk wind behind it, hence the observation that in North Wales, the rain falls horizontally.

Scotland comprises two mountain areas, with a central lowland valley in between the two. The south of Scotland is the gentler of the two and is moorland with some moderate peaks. The north is very obviously mountainous and, like the Lake District, is well set up to welcome visitors in the valleys and the lochs (lakes), but suited only for mountaineers on the higher ground.

The visitor should be made aware of daylight variation from season to season and from south to north. In the south, typically, the winter solstice will see daylight from 8am to 3.30pm and the summer solstice daylight from 4am to 10pm. This seasonal variation becomes more pronounced as one travels north, to the extent that, in Shetland, darkness lasts for only an hour or so in mid-summer – and it is not fully dark even then – but the position reverses itself in mid-winter. Most tourists will be here in the summer and, certainly, visitors who have travelled from countries further south can expect much longer daylight hours than they are used to at home.

Main Dates in English History

Date

BC 10,000   End of last Ice Age and probable time of reoccupation of
Britain

BC 8000   Probable date of separation of Britain and Europe

BC 55   1st Roman Invasion: Colchester established as provincial
capital

AD

45   2nd Roman invasion

60   Boudicca's rebellion

81   Battle of Mons Graupius: Agricola defeats the Picts

95-100   London becomes Provincial Capital

122   Work on Hadrian's Wall begins

212   Britain divided into two Provinces with capitals being
London and York.

410-425   Roman withdrawal

447-449   Saxon army arrives

490-500   Probable date of King Arthur's victory at Mons Badonicus

597   Arrival of St. Augustine's mission: reintroduction of
Christianity

663   Synod of Whitby: date of Easter settled by King
Oswiu of Northumberland.

754	Offa becomes King of Mercia and ruler of the Britons
782	Work begins on Offa's Dyke
780s	Late 780s Offa introduces the Penny, in silver
827	Egbert becomes first King of England
869	Viking conquest
880	Alfred the Great establishes navy.
1066	Battle of Stamford Bridge and Hastings, and the Norman invasion
1086	The Domesday Book
1150s	Establishment of jury trial
1170	Murder of Thomas à Becket
(1095-1200)	Crusades. Richard the Lionheart's success at the siege of Acre
1215	Magna Carta sealed at Runnymede, nr. Windsor, Berkshire
1225	Henry 3rd reissues the Magna Carta
1258	The Grand Council under the Provisions of Oxford: First House of Commons and the seeds of democracy
1282	Union of Wales and England
1295	First "model" Parliament
1296	Scots defeated at Dunbar: Balliol dethroned
1328	Independence for Scotland
1346	Battle of Crecy
(1347-50)	Black Death 1/3rd to 1/2 of population die
1356	Battle of Poitiers
1381	Peasants' Revolt
1415	Battle of Agincourt
1440-1485	Wars of the Roses
1452	Final loss of France
1474	Introduction of printing by William Caxton
1485	Battle of Bosworth. Henry Tudor crowned king
1492	Discovery of America by Christopher Columbus
1515	Henry VIII crowned king
1529	Fall of Cardinal Wolsey
1532	Henry VIII becomes Head of the Church in England

1539	Dissolution of the Monasteries
1553	Lady Jane Grey deposed
1563	Act of Supremacy
1564	Birth of William Shakespeare
1571	Introduction of tobacco
1588	Defeat of the Spanish Armada
1603	Crowns of England and Scotland united
1605	Gunpowder Plot
1620	Pilgrim Fathers leave Plymouth for America to found new colony
1640	Long Parliament
1644	Battle of Marston Moor
1645	Battle of Naseby
1649	Execution of Charles 1st
1645-1659	Commonwealth under Cromwell
1665	Great Plague
1666	Great Fire of London
1677	Prevention of Fraud Act establishes use of signature for validation of documents
1679	Habeas Corpus Act
1685	Battle of Sedgemoor, Bloody Assize
1688	Bloodless Revolution – William of Orange crowned
1689	Bill of Right
1690	Battle of the Boyne
1692	Massacre of Glencoe
1693	Origin of the National Debt
1704	Battle of Blenheim: Acquisition of Gibraltar
1707	Union of Scotland and England
1745	Charles defeated at Prestonpans
1746	Charles defeated at Culloden Moor
1752	Change from Julian Calendar to Gregorian Calendar
1756	Black Hole of Calcutta
1765	Stamp Act in America

1770	Discovery of Australia and New Zealand
	America declares Independence
1779	Ironbridge Gorge Bridge built
1780	Admiral Rodney defeats Spanish
1782	Great Britain cedes independence to America
1789	French Revolution
1800	Union of Ireland and Great Britain
1805	Battle of Trafalgar off the coast of Spain
1814	Wellington's victory at Toulouse
1815	Battle of Waterloo, south of Brussels. Napoleon finally defeated
1829	Catholic Emancipation
1833	Abolition of Slavery
1834	First invention of hard surfaced roads by Macadam.
1837	Queen Victoria crowned
1843	Start of the tea-clipper era, fast sailing boats bringing tea from China
1854/55	Crimean War, Battles of Alma, Balaclava, & Inkerman
1855	Fall of Sebastopol, end of Crimean War
1857	Indian Mutiny
1861-65	American Civil War
1862	Cotton Famine in Manchester
1870	Irish Land Act
1876	Invention of telephone by Alexander Bell
1885	Death of General Gordon at Khartoum
1886	Gladstone's Irish Home Rule Bill defeated
1890	Invention of compression ignition ("diesel") engine by Herbert Ackroyd-Stewart
1898	Battle of Omdurman: re-conquest of Sudan
1899-1900	Boer War in South Africa
1901	Queen Victoria dies: Perfection of "tarmacadam" road surfacing by Edward Purnell Hooley
1910	Balfour Declaration on Jewish Homeland

1911	Invention of television by Robert Alexander-Swinton
1914	World War 1 begins, Battle of the Aisne: defeat of Schleiffen Plan
1915	1st Battle of Ypres (Belgium)
1916	Battle of Somme (France)
1917	2nd and 3rd Battles of Ypres: Passchendale
1918	4th battle of Ypres: end of WW1 and the Armistice: 11th November 1918
1918	Representation of the People Act gives votes to women
1921	Independence for Ireland
1926	General Strike
1932	Great Depression
1933	Britain leaves the Gold Standard
1939	WW2 begins
1940	Dunkirk Rescue
	September – Battle of Britain victory
1945	End of World War 2
1953	June: Coronation of HM Queen Elizabeth 2nd

Britain

Many are confused by the various terms used in connection with Britain: the United Kingdom, Britain, Great Britain, the British Isles, England, Scotland, Northern Ireland (Ulster) and Wales. It may be useful to clarify what means what.

England, Northern Ireland (or Ulster), Scotland and Wales are the names of the constituent countries of the United Kingdom. The term "Great Britain" came into being when, in 1707, Queen Anne united England with Scotland. Prior to that, "Britain" meant – and still means – the old Roman province of Britannia: England and Wales. Subsequently, came the addition of Ireland and the many islands in the surrounding seas and some people found it easier to refer to the United Kingdom as a catch-all term to include the whole entity.

"The British Isles" means nothing different from Great Britain but merely emphasises the fact that the kingdom comprises not only the mainland but also the many offshore islands, including the Isles of Anglesey, Hebrides, Lundy, Man, Orkney, Shetland and Wight. Orkney and Shetland were once part of the kingdom of Denmark and became part of Scotland in the 15th Century.

The islands off Scotland are attractive to tourists for their wildlife, remoteness and tranquillity. However, the visitor should be made aware that, whatever means of travel is chosen, the journey will take at least two days. For example, a trip to Shetland will entail travel to Aberdeen followed by onward travel overnight by ferry or the next day by air. Most visitors to the Hebrides, Orkney or Shetland drive to a ferry terminal, then take the ferry. The ferry services are very good, but in most cases there is only one daily.

Britannia is the first name applied to this country, a name chosen by the Romans, but it may be a Latin version of a name already in existence: in his book "Britain Begins" Professor Sir Barry Cunliffe indicates that the ancient Britons described themselves as "Pretani". England is a derivative of angle-land, the Angles being one of the Germanic tribes who, in the 5th & 6th centuries, settled in this country. The name of Scotland is more complicated. Scots (or "Scotiae") is the name given by the Romans (again, probably just latin-ising the name they called themselves) to the tribes living in the north eastern corner of Ireland, loosely what is now Northern Ireland. Those living in the remainder of Ireland were given the name Hibernians (Hiberniae). Some of the Scots from north east Ireland migrated to southern Scotland in the 5th century and gradually took over the country, displacing the existing tribes living there, the Caledoniae and the Picti. The country subsequently became known as Scotland. The term "scotch" applies only to whisky: the people are Scots or Scottish.

England, Scotland, Northern Ireland and Wales remain separate countries, under one central government and one central monarchy, though Scotland has its own distinctive legal system. Northern Ireland, Scotland and Wales have their own regional governments, with powers devolved from Westminster. Queen Elizabeth 2nd is Queen of England, Scotland, Wales and Northern Ireland (Ulster). Southern Ireland (Eire) became independent in 1921 but the north – the ancient kingdom of Ulster – has a protestant majority which wanted to remain part of Great Britain. That view prevails to the present time, even though the Roman Catholic minority want Northern Ireland to become part of Eire, the Southern Irish Republic. The issue remains contentious.

Great Britain and its islands have a total land area of 94,525 square miles and a total population (2016) of 65,000,000. This population is unevenly distributed inasmuch as, for example Scotland, which has a population of 5,120,000 over some 30,000 square miles in area, Wales has 2,900,000 spread around 8,000 square miles whereas in England, 52,480,000 people live in the 50,436 square miles of its area. This population is heavily weighted towards the south eastern corner of the country, where, for example, the density of population is over 1600 to the square mile. Consequently, over-crowding and congestion are contentious issues.

Each of the constituent countries is sub-divided into counties or shires – each with its own county council – and some of the larger counties are sub-divided again to districts. Most towns and cities have their own town councils and all these councils have their own devolved powers. This is very much the legacy of our Saxon system of village, manor, town and king's moots or councils.

In 2014, Scotland held a referendum on independence and rejected it by a margin larger than expected but not so decisively that the issue can be deemed settled permanently. Consequently, the Westminster government is reviewing not only the relationship with Scotland but the political structure of the entire country. Proposals made so far suggest a more regionalised structure in which Wales and Scotland will gain more powers but will lose influence on English affairs.

History and Pre-History

It will be helpful if the reader has a clear understanding of what is history and what is pre-history. Pre-history is the period before there were written records and history is the period afterwards. We can say that pre-history is discovered from archaeology and history is discovered from written records, although there is a great deal of overlap. Ancient burial sites and graves have been known to yield information over and above that which historians have discovered from documentary evidence. It may seem a strange concept, but this book could become out of date: a further discovery, perhaps from archaeological evidence or even from previously undiscovered documents could overturn and completely change our ideas of what occurred in the past. History itself may be fixed but our understanding of it is not.

In the case of Britain, that means that for practical purposes, history began with the arrival of the Romans, although some written artefacts have been found which date before that time. Literacy seems to have been widespread during Roman times: inscriptions and notes written by ordinary soldiers have been found. That said, the situation is complicated by the severe contraction in literacy which took place between the departure of the Romans and the reintroduction of Christianity, in AD 597 via King Aethelbert, King of Kent. Even after that date, literacy – and written records, outside the kings' courts – was restricted largely to the church and the monasteries. Early history is normally taken to mean the time from the arrival of the Romans until the

Norman Conquest in AD 1066. The period from then onwards until about 1500 AD is generally referred to as the mediaeval period, from 1500 – 1600 the Tudor Period, and events after 1600 are regarded as modern history.

BRITISH HISTORY IN BRIEF

In Ancient Times

Before the arrival of the Romans, Britain was inhabited by scores of what are usually referred to as "Celtic" tribes, most of them living in the upper valleys of rivers, where the soils were lighter and easier to plough. At that time, the only plough available was the shoulder plough, pushed by one man, which limited the ground that could be cultivated to chalky soils inland and the sandy soils of eastern England. The term Celtic is a catch-all term intended to include almost every tribe in western Europe. The exception is those living in eastern Kent – the Cantiae – who were described as "Belgic" tribes, originating from the southern part of the low countries.

These early inhabitants were relatively sophisticated people who crossed to the European mainland from time to time and conducted trading and social relations with the various tribal groups there. A reader who wishes to learn more of the early population and development since the last ice age should read Sir Barry Cunliffe's brilliant book, *Britain Begins*. Indeed, readers may be surprised how much of our history and pre-history has been pieced together over the last half century, thanks to the work not only of historians but also of archaeologists, forensic scientists and geneticists. Of course, while written records (usually) give us certainty – and a much more complete picture – historians have to be wary of the easy presumption that, merely because a document is ancient, it provides a guarantee of reliability. Even the most seemingly respectable document needs to be read with a sceptical eye.

The ancient Britons left behind a number of mysteries, in particular, stone circles. The two best known stone circles are at Stonehenge, Wiltshire – on the A303, the main road between Andover and Wincanton – and at Avebury, Wiltshire, on the road between Swindon and Devizes. It has been established that the stones were brought from a huge distance away and both were in use for many centuries. However, it is not known what these circles signified, what they were used for or whether their primary purpose was religious, social or political. An equally interesting but less dramatic stone circle is to be found at Little Rollright, near Chipping Norton, Oxfordshire, on the border with Gloucestershire.

According to Professor Cunliffe, it is probable that Britain was re-occupied about 10,000BC as the ice of the last Ice Age retreated. Because of proximity to the Ice Pack, the various Ice Ages saw occupation, evacuation and reoccupation as the population retreated before the advancing ice, then advanced northward as it retreated. As it retreated for the last time, meltwater from the glaciers and flows from the rivers were unable to escape quickly enough and around 8,000BC the rising waters breached the land bridge between Britain and Europe. Thus Britain became an island.

The Romans

First, a note on the names of Romans. The first name is a given (or "Christian") name, the second the family name. The third is a cognomen or epithet describing a characteristic of the individual or family. It might be useful to think of it as a nickname. Thus the individual we know as Julius Caesar was, actually, Caius, or Gaius – given name; Julius – family name; Caesar, descriptive name conferred when he became Caesar, or Dictator.

The Roman Army General and Provincial Governor of Gaul (France), Caius Julius – later Julius Caesar – was troubled by constant rebellion. Convinced that the Belgic tribes in East Kent, as well as some of the other tribes in the south east corner of England, were aiding and abetting the rebellion, he invaded southern England in 55BC, with the intention of creating a cordon sanitaire. He landed at Richborough (1) and conquered the south eastern corner of England. He also learned a very hard lesson: the seas around England are nowhere near as benign as those of the Mediterranean. This is particularly true of what we now call the English Channel, which is subject to extremely vigorous tidal movements. The cause of this is that two large bodies of tidal water, the North Sea and Atlantic Ocean, are connected by the English Channel which tapers towards the Strait of Dover, at its narrowest point only 21 miles across. On a clear day, from the cliffs at Dover, it is possible to see the other side quite easily. (And the Dover Cliffs can be seen clearly from the beach at Sangatte, on the French coast.) To avoid the worst of these tides, he set up the provincial capital at Colchester, Essex (2). Colchester was a reasonably convenient spot: it had the advantage of being a safe and sheltered landing, upstream away from sea-storms and, being further north, the longer, wider crossing was easier for shipping to cope with, compared to the short sea crossing where the tidal movements are most difficult. It was already an established tribal centre for the region. Having created his cordon sanitaire, Caius Julius brought it under the control of a military administration with a suitable garrison, but did nothing further. In fact, beyond administering the area, the Romans did nothing more for 100 years until, in 45AD, Appius Claudius Pulcher – Claudius the Fair – decided to explore the entire country, conquering as he went, naturally. There were two motives behind this. First, a good military record was an invaluable asset for any rising officer of the Roman army, and the tribes beyond the boundaries of the empire were useful track-record fodder. At that time, the Roman army was the most highly organised, trained, disciplined and powerful army in the world and barbarian tribes were no match. His second motive was to find out what assets were to be found in this country and what value they might be to the empire. Increasing the wealth of the Roman Empire – or, at least, of Rome – was important and, again, would be helpful to the career of anyone ambitious.

At that time, three Roman cities had been founded under Julius Caesar: Verulamium (St Albans) (3), Londinium (London) and Camulodunum (Colchester). Then in AD60, a group of Roman army auxiliaries in East Anglia ran amok and murdered Prasutagus, king of the East Anglian Iceni tribe, then raped his queen and his daughters. Unfortunately, that queen was Boudicca (Boadicea) and she rallied other tribes into an alliance which rebelled against Roman rule. It should be suspected that some sort of conspiracy to resist was already in the making, if only because it would have been pretty much impossible to have assembled such an alliance in such a short space of time. She came close to breaking Roman control: she destroyed a complete Roman legion then went on to destroy Colchester, St Albans and London and its bridge. London was particularly important because it was the site of a strategic bridge – the furthest downstream on the river - and its destruction would prevent Roman reinforcements in the south from crossing the River Thames. Eventually, the provincial governor, Gaius Suetonius Paulinus, defeated her in battle at a location thought to be near Hinckley, not far from where the Fosse Way crosses Watling Street – the A5, a Roman road which runs from London to Holyhead, Anglesey. The Fosse Way is another old Roman road which runs from Lincoln to Bath. Large stretches of both still exist within the present-day road network; in places part of a major highway, in some, a minor road and occasionally as a footpath but they are traceable on maps. Historian John Waite has written *Boudicca's Last Stand*, an excellent book on the subject of this rebellion, and may have identified the exact location of that final battle.

As the Romans expanded the area under their control, they built roads, not for wheeled traffic primarily, though they did have carts and chariots, but in order to march troops from one place to another. They also built forts as secure stopping places along these routes. A day's march would have been about 20 miles (32Km). With the aid of a road map of Britain, it is quite possible to identify some of those roads even today, in spite of progress. Roman roads are noticeably straight. The road between London and Canterbury –the A2 (4) and between London and North Wales – the A5 – are among the most easily identified. The Romans left us with a standard military measure of distance: the mile. Milia is the Latin word meaning thousands and miles means soldier. If you pace out left-right-left, you move forward just over 5 feet (1.52m) or roughly a yard and three-quarters. A thousand of those is 1760 yards, or one mile. The Roman standard pace is shorter than ours – they were shorter people, of course: a Roman mile is 1619 yards, (1.5Km) or 0.92 of an imperial mile.

Roman explorations extended as far as the north coast of Scotland and they fought a number of battles against the natives (not the Scots: more of this later) culminating in the battle of Mons Graupius in AD81. Under the generalship of Gnaeus Julius Agricola, the Roman army won this battle decisively and killed some 20,000 of the enemy's army of 30,000. It did Agricola's reputation little good, for back in Rome, the Senate was appalled that he had allowed 10,000 of the enemy to escape.

Roman Main Towns and Roads

Hadrians Wall

York

Lincoln

Chester

Colchester

Cirencester

St Albans

London

Canterbury

Exeter

The Romans decided not to incorporate Scotland into the Roman Empire. This was essentially a commercial decision inasmuch as Rome considered that it would cost more to conquer and keep subdued than it would yield in wealth. The Roman Empire had by that time adopted a practice of building walls marking the boundary of the Empire and intended to do so in Britannia. The first wall was built in the central valley of Scotland, loosely between Edinburgh and Glasgow – the Antonine Wall. Subsequently, a wall was built across southern Scotland – and finally, on the directions of the then emperor, Hadrian, the wall from Newcastle to Carlisle now known as Hadrian's Wall (5). Large sections of this last wall survive to this day, along with many of the various camps, castles, customs entrances and settlements that were necessary in a military area. Tourists wanting to explore the wall are well catered for and some informative lectures are provided from time to time.

Around AD95-100, the then provincial governor, probably Aulus Plautius Nepos, moved the provincial capital from Colchester to London. It was purely a matter of expedience of where the governor located his office and that of his civil servants, all of whom – including the governor himself – were on three-year postings. By this time several developments had taken place. First, London had become a major trading post and port and was securely fortified. Second, with the area of Britain under Roman control now much expanded, the bureaucracy had grown and there was a constant stream of legates, messengers, civil servants and governors travelling between London and Rome. By then, the Romans had learned some of the techniques necessary to cope with the riptides for which the English Channel is notorious, so London became a more convenient embarkation point.

From then on, the settlement became much more militarised and by 200 AD, fortification around the boundary of London reached the point where it had become a walled city. Parts of the Roman city walls can still be found, the best examples being adjacent to the Tower of London and at London Wall (6).

Soldiers in the Roman army enlisted for 20 years, nominally on bachelor status, and on completion of service were given enough land to support themselves as farmers. These farming communities of retired soldiers were known as coloniae – colonies.

In the 4th century, the activities of pirates – Saxons, Vikings and many others – caused sufficient concern to the military authorities to warrant serious action, so patrol ships known as pictae were put to sea to monitor and inhibit pirates and to deter them from raiding the English mainland. Pictae were stained in a sea green colour to make them difficult to see. The term Pictae means no more than something which is painted, stained or dyed. This military maritime force might raise the question of whether King Alfred the Great truly was the father of the navy, although we should remember that the pictae were ships of the Roman army not of the British.

The Saxon Settlements, King Arthur and St. Patrick

Exactly when the Roman army withdrew from England is uncertain. It was probably a gradual process, but we can be quite certain that by AD 425 withdrawal was complete. The country was left exposed: a prosperous place with the Roman army safely out of the way was an obvious target for raids. The country was attacked from all directions and was militarily helpless – even those who knew how to wage war had little idea how to command an army. The Roman army enlisted locals as troopers and possibly junior officers, but not as army commanders. Generally, legionnaires were not stationed in their home country. England was easy prey. At some point in the late 440s, a local chieftain, Vortigen or Wehrtgern, brought over an army of Saxons as mercenaries. That army is said to have been led by Hengist and his brother, Horsa. Hengist translates as "stallion" and Horsa as "horse", so these may be nicknames rather than actual names. They landed at Ebbsfleet near Gravesend (7) in AD 447. Payment for these mercenaries was probably in land but, whatever it was, the arrangement went sour and the Saxons mutinied. Horsa was killed in battle at Aylesford, shortly afterwards. Word went back home that resistance from the natives was weak and the country was open for the taking. That led to three closely related tribes migrating to England. They were the Angles from Angeln, just over the present border in Denmark, the Jutes from the Baltic coast of Germany, and the Saxons from the lowland areas of northern Germany and the Netherlands now referred to as Friesland, Saxony and Schleswig-Holstein. The Saxons were originally known as "frissones" – frisians. They migrated family by family, village by village, penetrating the interior via the river valleys. Where they found suitable land, they settled; if locals were already there, they evicted or killed them. Indeed, some historians suggest that the ancient Britons did not survive the onslaught, although it is reasonable to suppose that even if the men were killed, some of the women survived as wives or slaves for the new settlers. If the English have even a little ancient Briton blood in them, it is almost certainly of distaff origin –the female side of the family tree.

Early Saxon Settlements

King Arthur

We now come to the legend of King Arthur, a shadowy figure of whom we know very little. He is surrounded by almost limitless myth and legend, but only a little reliable history. We know nothing about his being a king, although he might have been offered kingship as a reward for his military successes. He certainly was not King of Wessex: that was a Saxon kingdom that came into being some 100 years later. He is, however, associated with the West Country, which subsequently became known as Wessex. Nor yet did he live in a stone castle: castles of that kind were not to appear for another 600 years. That said, the remains of a very large wooden fortification have been found at Pendoggett, not far from Tintagel and close to the valley of the River Camel in Cornwall (8). The fort is known locally as Tregeare Rounds or Castle Dameliock. It is about the right age and must have been something special, for it is too large – some 450 yards (411m) in diameter – and too heavily fortified for any normal secure stockade. It has been suggested that this might have been Camelot, but there is no hard evidence. Additionally, there is a grave site within Glastonbury Abbey (9) which is said to have been the grave of King Arthur but, again, verification has proved impossible.

We have only two written records relating to Arthur, one being a copy of the other. The original work is that of Gildas the Wise, a monk who lived from 504 – 570 AD, so his lifetime might have overlapped that of this Arthur figure. Later, the venerable Bede (lived AD 673–735) – a monk at Wearmouth monastery (10)

–included much of Gildas' work in his own *"Ecclesiastical History of the English People"*, completed in AD 731. In Gildas' work, *On the ruination of Britain,* he describes "Arthur" as a Roman of good but not noble birth, whose family were killed by the Saxons, he being the sole survivor. Gildas gives him the name Ambrosius Aurelianus. This gives us a clue to where the name "Arthur" might have come from. He might have been referred to as one having skill or talent, in which case he could have been referred to as Ambrosius Aurelianus Artorius. Equally, it might have come from the word utu or ata, the ancient Briton word meaning horrible bear. Arthur would have had three major advantages over the Saxons: familiarity with the Roman road network, which would have enabled him to move troops quickly and, probably, knowledge of how to use horses in battle, a huge advantage which the Saxons had not, at that stage, learned. He would also have provided his soldiers with body armour, which the Saxons did not use, so their battle losses would have been invariably higher.

It is likely that there were many battles between the ancient Britons and the Saxons but one that we know about with some certainty is the battle of Mons Badonicus. The site has not been positively identified but is thought to be Baddesdown Hill near Bath (11). This was a decisive victory for Arthur and one which forced the Saxons to remain for some forty years to the east of the Fosse Way (12), an old Roman road which runs south west from Lincoln to Bath. It is still traceable on modern road maps. Arthur is said to have died subsequently at the battle of Camlann, some twenty-one years after the Battle of Mons Badonicus. The site of this battle likewise remains to be identified, but his enemy is said to have been called Medraut, a name which suggests that he might have been one of Arthur's own officers, implying dissension within the army. The Battle of Camlann is thought to have taken place around 510-511AD, which suggests that the Battle of Mons Badonicus would have been around 490AD.

Two of the myths relating to Arthur should, perhaps, be explained. First the drawing of the sword from the stone is a metaphor of the steel-making process, in which ironstone is mined from underground rocks and iron extracted. The myth of the Lady of the Lake is a reference to a practice among ancient Britons, which the Saxons are thought to have adopted later. When a notable warrior died – especially in battle – his sword was taken and then placed in water – a river or a lake – where, of course, it would rust. To the ancient Britons, the warrior's sword was being returned to the earth, from whence it came.

The Angles, Saxons and Jutes were rural, lowland people who lived in wooden buildings. They were terrified by Roman towns and suspected that evil spirits lived there. A typical Anglo-Saxon house was single roomed, split timber building over a pit, which was then filled with sand. This kept the floor fairly dry and enabled them to keep a fire burning in the centre. Somewhere very close to the village, there would have been a fortified stockade, where women and children would go in times of danger. This stockade was called a burr – hence our use of the word borough or burgh.

In rough terms, the Angles settled in the east of England, the Saxons to the south and west and the Jutes, Hampshire and the Isle of Wight. The island is named after one of their chieftains – Wightig. All Saxon chieftains and, later, kings, claimed descent from their god of war, Woden, pronounced Voden or Foden.

The early years after the Saxons arrived are sometimes referred to as the Dark Ages because we know relatively little about those times and what information we do have has been hard to come by. Literacy – and, consequently written records – almost disappeared until the return of Christianity, which came about because, in 597 AD Pope Gregory the Great sent a monk called Augustine as head of a group of some 40 missionaries to the King of Kent, Aethelbert. Aethelbert was married to Bertha, who happened to be Christian, so Aethelbert was receptive and readily converted. Land was provided in what is now Canterbury for a centre for the mission and, from then on, the return of Christianity spread steadily throughout England. Canterbury became the centre of Christianity in Britain and remains so to this day.

St. Patrick is another shadowy figure from the Saxon era, said to have lived during the 6th century. There is a view in some historical circles that he was a slave trader and most historians agree that he was an ancient Briton or, more likely, a Saxon of a wealthy family. It is known that he lived on the family farm, just south of Solway Firth, near Carlisle. He was kidnapped by pirates and taken to what is now the Republic of Ireland (Eire). Eventually, he managed to escape, and he was greatly helped by the local people. On his return home, he studied for the priesthood and upon completion of his studies, returned to Ireland to bring Christianity to the island, as a gesture of gratitude for the assistance given in making his escape. He later became the patron saint of Ireland.

Saxon society evolved into what is known as the manorial system. The regional king was deemed to "own" the land and rented out sections of it to lords of the manor. Lords of the manor rented to lesser landholders and so on. Later on, it became common for kings to give estates to the church or to monasteries, so that rents would provide them with an income. The basic unit of land, known as a hide, was a unit on which a family could live and feed itself. A typical hide would have been about 45 acres but, necessarily, this would have varied, depending on the quality of the land and its resulting yields. The hide-holder, who may even have owned his land, would have paid three main taxes to his lord: church-scot, for the maintenance of the church; bridge-scot for the maintenance of paths and bridges; and land-scot or food-rent. From this derives our expression "scot-free" – free of tax or charge: nothing to do with Scotland or Scotsmen. The last of these taxes was quite often paid to the lord of the manor in labour, by working in his fields one or two days each week. Bearing in mind that the hide-holder had to work on his own land as well, his was a demanding imposition but not unbearable.

Saxon society also gave us our modern system of local and national government. Each village would meet regularly to resolve or decide disputes and to make decisions about local administration. This was called the village moot and its fundamental principle was that the landholders were deemed to have as many rights against their lord as he had against them. Above this village moot, there would have been a manorial moot, which operated in much the same way. Finally, at the top of the tree was the King's moot or Witan, where matters affecting the entire kingdom were decided. From this we get our expression "mooted", i.e. something suggested or put forward for discussion.

There then began a process of coalescence which continued unevenly until the 11th Century as Angle, Saxon and Jute tribes conquered each other's territories and married the daughters of other chieftains. Consequently, tribal kingdoms expanded or were subsumed into others. For example, the counties of Essex, Surrey and Kent were, at one point, independent kingdoms. However, by AD 600, Anglo-Saxon kingdoms had become noticeably larger and fewer. Angle, Saxon and Jutish kings gradually fell into a hierarchy of senior kings and lesser kings, and by about AD750 the title Bretwalda had emerged: this had applied to senior kings with authority beyond the borders of their own kingdoms but came eventually to mean the most senior king, the king of kings. The best known of these was Offa, King of Mercia (loosely, the Midlands, with the royal centre at Tamworth, Staffordshire) (13). In royal documents and charters, Offa described himself as King of Mercia and ruler of all the Britons. Offa is remembered for three things in particular: Offa's Dyke (13) – the ditch and mound some 185 miles long which he ordered to be constructed to determine the boundary between his realm and those of the Welsh lords – and the penny, named after his ancestor Penda, which he introduced and which remains part of our currency to this day. Actually, he introduced a whole system of coinage, which survived for generations after him. Finally, a few months before he died in AD796, Offa concluded the first Trade Treaty ever signed in Europe, with Charlemagne, King of the Franks. It records that England had an advanced textile trade at the time. After Offa died, his two sons were unable to hold the wide authority of their father and seniority – and with it the title Bretwalda slipped away to the kings of Wessex. In 827AD, Egbert, King of Wessex, conquered the south of England, Mercia and East Anglia and then persuaded Northumbria – a term then meaning everywhere north of the Humber – to submit. Thus Egbert became the first true King of England.

The Vikings

In many ways, the incursions of the Vikings from Denmark and Scandinavia were a repeat of those of the Angles and Saxons. They came from an adjacent area, the island of Gotland and Southern Sweden, though they had by that time spread their territory to Norway and the islands between Sweden and Denmark. The first Viking raids were recorded in AD787 as mere plunder but, inevitably, they became bolder and ventured further inland. By degrees, they eventually began to settle and by AD 869 they had conquered the east and north east of England. At the time, it was feared they might conquer the whole country. It was Alfred, grandson of King Egbert, who resisted the Vikings and who pressed them back, preventing complete takeover. It was not long before the Danes, led by Guthrun, attacked again, reaching Wessex. A long campaign ensued ending in the Treaty of Wedmore in AD 878, in which England was divided into the south and west, ruled by Alfred and the north and east, ruled by the Vikings. This northern and eastern area became known as Danelagh or Danelaw.

One Viking settlement is at what became known as Jorvik – now known as York (14) – which had been an important settlement under the Romans and the Saxons. Part of the Viking settlement has been discovered and partly restored. The Yorvik museum, just behind Coppergate, is now open to the public.

Alfred's skill in preventing the Vikings from taking over the whole country gave him the status of a great statesmen and the title, "the Great". There were, however, further groups of Vikings who raided the country, and Alfred's response was to establish a fleet of ships, said to be more formidable than those of the Vikings, to patrol the North Sea coast and to take on any raiding parties before they reached land. This was an effective deterrent and earned Alfred the further title: Father of the Royal Navy, for this was the first formation of a British maritime fighting force intended exclusively for battle at sea.

Alfred's subsequent rule encouraged literacy and learning, and he is regarded as the father of English prose. His son, Edward the Elder, managed to re-conquer much of Danelaw up to the Humber and Eadred, Alfred's grandson, built on this work to re-conquer the whole country and bring it under Saxon rule once more. There then followed a period of relative calm under King Edgar – whose queen, Elfrida, is the first recorded crowned queen of England – but after Edgar's death, the peace and calm ended abruptly. In AD 978, the new King Edward died at Corfe Castle (15) and murder was suspected, with Elfrida often being portrayed as the culprit. Edward was replaced by Aethelred or Ethelred, who was a disastrous ruler. He quickly acquired the epithet "the Unread" – a pun on his name, but which reflected the Saxon view of him, "the Unfit". We know him as Ethelred the Unready. He was incapable of keeping his nobles united and the Danes, seeing weakness and disharmony in the country, recommenced their raids. Instead of defending his realm, Aethelred tried to buy them off with gifts known as Danegeld. Unsurprisingly, this had the opposite effect: it encouraged the raids. A saying of the time was "If you pay the danegeld, you never get rid of the Dane".

Aethelred then made the situation even worse by resorting to treachery. Having once made a truce with the Danes he then, in AD1002, ordered the murder of the sister and brother-in-law of the Danish king (Sweyn), as well as all the Danes he could reach. Bringing down on the country the full might of the Danish army, he then fled to Normandy and was replaced by Edmund. Edmund resisted the onslaught of the Danish armies but was betrayed by

Edric, formerly a favourite of Aethelred. That caused his defeat and, shortly afterwards, his murder. That brought, in AD1016, the Dane, Knut to the English throne.

Knut actually turned out to be a good ruler, joining the two royal lines by marrying Queen Emma, the widow of Aethelred the Unready. There is a tale about Knut (sometimes spelt Canute) commanding the tide to turn back. There is truth in the tale, but it was intended as a rebuke to some of his sycophantic courtiers and intended to prove that even the might of a king could not reverse the waves.

The Normans

Knut died in 1035 and neither of his sons lived long so in 1042, a new king had to be chosen by the Witan and that choice fell on Edward, second son of Aethelred. Edward was a pious, slightly unworldly individual who had something of a fetish for all things Norman. Once crowned, he appointed a Norman as Archbishop of Canterbury and several bishops, which made him unpopular in the country. His one memorial is that almost immediately after his coronation he began work on the building of Westminster Abbey. His fondness of the Normans enabled William of Normandy to claim that Edward had promised the English throne to him. This may or may not have been true: William made the same claim about other kingdoms and dukedoms. Edward died in 1066.

William of Normandy was the son of the Duke of Normandy, Robert "the Devil". Duke Robert had a long-standing relationship with Matilda, the daughter of a furrier. The difference in rank made marriage impossible, so when William was born, he was illegitimate and known as William the Bastard.

Back in England, the English Witan wanted a strong ruler who would stand up to the Danes and chose Harold, son of the Saxon earl Godwin. At that point, William made his claim and then Harold's brother Tostig (who also claimed the throne) landed in Northumbria (16) with the King of Norway and an army of Norse warriors. Harold had little choice but to march northwards with his army, to meet them. They met at the battle of Stamford Bridge (17), near York. It resulted in a crushing victory for Harold which settled the Scandinavian question finally. Of the three hundred ships which had made landfall, twenty-four were sufficient to carry home the survivors.

Meanwhile, one hundred and fifty miles to the south, William of Normandy made his move and landed at Hastings, on the Kent coast. William had spent some time planning his invasion at Le Mans – now better known for its famous motor race – and where, 90 years later in 1154, Henry 2nd was born. Consequently, King Harold had to march his men south to meet them. The view is often expressed that Harold made several avoidable mistakes. Certainly, he did not replace the men he had lost at Stamford Bridge and those he marched south would undoubtedly have benefited from rest. It might be that, flushed with success, Harold thought himself invincible. Whatever the truth of that might be, Harold met the Normans at Battle (18), just north of Hastings, on 14th October 1066 and went straight into battle. For most of the day, Harold's optimism appeared well founded but a feint by the Norman forces led to an ill judged move by Harold, which left his army exposed to the Norman cavalry, and they cut the Saxons to pieces and won the day. Actually, Harold might well still have won, had he himself not been killed, supposedly by an arrow through the eye. The resulting loss of morale among the Saxon army was the final straw. The battlefield and a commemorative abbey built on the orders of William – Battle Abbey – are still there to be seen beside the A2100 road, just north of Hastings. From that time until 1400, the kings of England were foreigners – Normans or Frenchmen.

The country did not submit immediately and, indeed, another king – Edgar – was chosen to succeed Harold, but eventually the country did submit to William. Now known as "the Conqueror" – at least, in his presence – William was never completely certain of his hold on the country and he often resorted to brutality and terror to enforce his will. As a result, many of the changes he made were to strengthen his grip on power. His first move was to declare all those who had fought at Hastings to be outlaws, which enabled him to take the estates of the nobles and hand them to his favourites – or those of his army he felt the need to keep on-side.

The feudal system associated with Norman rule was not, actually, very different from the existing Saxon manorial system but it was imposed with much more cruelty. That is not particularly surprising. The new nobles had been given feudal power over a conquered people whom they hated, and they were anxious to make the most of their new-found lands. There were obligations that went with these estates but, here again, they were not vastly different from what had gone before. They were, however, more easily ignored where they gave rights to the manorial tenants. The nobles were obliged to fight for the king if required and to bring men along with them. In turn, their tenants had to serve their respective Norman lords in much the same way that they had served their Saxon lords, but their duties were much more burdensome.

The main changes made by William were that several church dioceses were altered geographically, and Norman bishops appointed. Apart from that, estates were kept largely intact, but most were in Norman hands. Indeed, William, probably suffering from an inferiority complex resulting from his illegitimacy, was never completely confident of his grip on the country. That affected the changes he made and the awards of estates only to people who were trusted completely. For the people, manorial duties and taxes were much more demanding but, essentially, they went to a Norman lord rather than a Saxon one. However, in assessing what taxes ought to be due to the Crown, it became apparent that little was known about the values and yields of the great estates, or even the number of men on them who might serve in an army should the country be invaded – indeed, it was the threat of invasion from Denmark that drew this to William's attention. He set out to have the country assessed and sent out his courtiers to discover and record the main details of each estate. The result was the Domesday Book of 1086. (19)

One remaining Norman contribution to modern English, which does not occur in other European languages, is the difference in terms between an animal and its meat. For example, a pig (in French, le porc) is pork when butchered, a sheep (le mouton) is mutton and a bull (le boeuf) is beef when served as meat. This developed because the peasant in his fields saw them only as animals whereas the lord, in his manor house, saw them only as meat and used the French Norman terms. The different terms have survived.

William the Conqueror died in 1087 as a result of injuries sustained in a riding accident. His son, known as William Rufus – rufus because of his red hair and beard – ascended to the throne. Compared with his father, he was much more autocratic, fat, greedy and even more unjust. He was also, almost certainly, homosexual. Consequently, he never married and when, in 1099 he was killed by a stray arrow while hunting in the New Forest (20), he had no heir, so the crown passed to Henry, brother of Duke Robert of Normandy.

Henry was a strong, autocratic king and a strict disciplinarian. It was common for him to order the severing of the right hand of anyone he thought guilty of stealing from him. Indeed, the only popular thing he did was to marry Matilda of Scotland, who was descended from the kings of Wessex. Even that was not well received immediately by the ruling class, who considered that marrying a Saxon – a race they despised – quite beneath royalty.

When Henry died in 1135, he was succeeded by the grandson of William the Conqueror – Stephen, who was a radically different character: a mild man indeed. It was widely hoped that he would make a more bearable king than the two Williams and Henry. Unfortunately, Maud, the late King Henry's daughter, thought that she should reign, despite having married Geoffrey of Anjou (21). The result was civil war, which resulted in a temporary victory for Maud's forces and put her on the throne, as Lady of England, for a very short period. She was never crowned and was quickly deposed, and civil war began again. England was, in effect, ruled by the barons and they ruled very badly. King Stephen then brought over a mercenary army whose behaviour was even worse. Stephen's reign was known as the reign of nineteen long winters. Stephen died in 1154, to be succeeded by Henry 2nd – the first of the Plantagenets. The Plantagenets were so called because Henry's ancestor, Geoffrey of Anjou – the area around Angers in the Loire Valley in France – wore a sprig of broom in his cap. The epithet was passed on to his successors.

Henry's first task was to restore order and to take control from the barons, which he did. He established a series of courts held by travelling judges who reinforced the king's law. A novel feature of these courts was that all who attended were seated. The French word for seated is "assis" and the courts are still known as "assizes". Henry also introduced the concept of juries – a body of men who would listen to cases and to give an opinion as to whether a defendant was guilty or not guilty – a system we have even unto this day.

Henry also rebuilt royal estates, took back the monopoly of coinage production, which put an end to private wars. The people supported him because, as a consequence, they lived under a unified law, with consistent justice and they found this infinitely better than the rule of the barons. One difficulty was that William the Conqueror had given the church power to apply its own laws to all who served the church in some way, not just clerics. A layman who committed murder would be hanged but scores of churchmen had committed murders since Henry's accession and had been spared: the church had no power to apply such a punishment. To bring the church back into line and under his power, Henry appointed his Chancellor, Thomas à Becket, as Archbishop of Canterbury. Becket, however, had ideas of his own, and became both pious and independent. In particular, Becket feared that, if priests were judged by the king's law, it would weaken the power of the church. Henry, not to be defied, drove Becket into exile. Six years later, Becket was allowed to return on condition that he fell into line. Becket did not keep his side of the bargain. Provoked in 1170 by Becket's opposition to his power over the church, Henry was heard, in exasperation, to remark "Who will rid me of this turbulent priest?". Four knights who overheard this outburst followed Becket to Canterbury Cathedral (22) and, once inside, hacked him to pieces by the steps of the altar. The country was horrified and considered Henry responsible for it. He served penance at Becket's tomb. Henry 2nd subsequently died in 1189 to be replaced by Richard the Lionheart.

Richard the Lionheart and the Crusades

Richard the Lionheart, often referred to as the Angevin King – the King of Anjou, loosely, what we now know as western and south western France – was probably the most foreign king of all, one who spent no more than seven months of his entire reign in England but who raised the standing of England and the English, particularly as warriors. He himself was noted for his personal courage, hence the tag "Lionheart".

At the instigation of Pope Urban in 1095, French forces had set off to help the forces of Christianity in their efforts to recover the Holy Land. Much of North Africa and the Holy Land had been under Arab – and therefore Islamic – rule since 690 AD. The Holy Land was ruled by the Fatimid caliphate, which had been reasonably tolerant of the Jewish and Christian religions. That changed in 1004 under Caliph al-Hakim, who is thought to have been insane. His worst act, from a European standpoint, was to have destroyed the Church of the Holy Sepulchre, one of the triggers which resulted in the European invasions known as the Crusades. That said, the first Crusade was triggered by a pope with an ulterior motive. Urban was engaged in a power struggle with the Emperor of Germany and needed to reassert the authority of Rome. Urban called upon the west to take arms against the Islamic forces that had conquered large swathes of the Middle East.

Most of the Crusades were French affairs and, indeed, the Caliphate soldiers referred to their European enemies as "Franks". In 1187, Richard the Lionheart and his men went on the third Crusade with the prime purpose of retaking the city of Acre, then moving on to Jerusalem. The Crusaders had the city under siege but were failing until Richard's bold and courageous leadership saved the day and the city fell. Many of the French army then went home, abandoning the secondary objective to retaking Jerusalem. Richard led his army to the Holy City but, having concluded that it was impregnable – and even if taken, probably could not be held – negotiated a peace settlement with Saleh al-Din (Saladin) which allowed access to the Holy City for Christian pilgrims, unaware that Saladin's forces were themselves exhausted and preparing to evacuate the city. In poor health, he himself then returned home, anxious to prevent his brother John and the Capetian king, Philip Augustus, from carving up his kingdom between them. On the way, he was shipwrecked and continued his journey over land, only to be taken prisoner by the Duke of Austria and held for some time. Meanwhile, his brother John had taken the throne, telling the country that Richard had been killed. Richard's return deposed John but, no sooner home and his crown reclaimed than Richard was off to war again, this time in France. While besieging the castle of Chaluz, he took an arrow in his neck – which he could have avoided – and he died of septicaemia.

King John and the Magna Carta

John re-took the crown but his weakness lost all his overseas territories, hence his nickname, Lackland. Even when compared with Aethelread the Unread, John is still considered the most disastrous king ever to reign: he was weak, devious, and treacherous – feared but never respected. The situation was made worse by the enormous pressure placed on Royal officials to raise funds to finance King John's wars, aimed at regaining these lost overseas possessions. Proving the axiom that desperate people do desperate things, the main collectors of revenues, the reeves and foresters, adopted some highly dubious practices in contriving offences and extracting fines. Eventually, this caused uproar amongst the barons, who forced John to carry out an investigation into the activities and methods of the tax collectors. Of course, King John knew perfectly well what was going on and attempted to backtrack, but eventually had to appoint 10 knights in every shire to "discover the evil practices of the sheriffs and foresters and prohibit them". The effect was to reduce royal revenues considerably and the king tried to reinstate the malpractices that had been so efficient in the recent past. The barons responded in AD 1215, by rebellion, then calling – perhaps summoning – the king to a meeting with them at Runnymeade, near Old Windsor, (23) where he was presented with and forced to seal the Magna Carta. At that time, legal documents and charters were not signed but sealed, using a seal impression unique to the individual or authority. The holder of that seal would normally carry the seal with him, to prevent it being used by anyone else. The Magna Carta established two great principles of law: that the king can take no tax without the common consent of the realm (now by vote of Parliament, effectively the same thing) and that no-one can be imprisoned or punished except after trial by equals – the right to trial by jury. It also bound the King to the law of the land, establishing the important principle of the Rule of Law. It did not establish democracy: that was to come 43 years later. There was a subsequent and slightly different version of the Magna Carta, in 1225, the latter being still treated as the definitive version and a constitutional reference to this day. Salisbury Cathedral, Lincoln Cathedral and the National Archive Library have a copy of the 1215 version; the 1225 version can be seen in the British Library and in Durham Cathedral, which has copies of all three charters: 1215, 1225 and 1300.

John then tried to circumvent the Magna Carta – even have it set aside – and that started a civil war which was stopped by his sudden death in 1216. His successor, Henry 3rd, was a boy at the time of his accession, but upon achieving manhood, he reigned badly. He was impulsive, puerile and gullible. He reissued and developed the Magna Carta in 1225 but failed to live up to it. That led to Simon de Montfort, a baron disgusted by the king's misdeeds, to call in 1258, a Great Council and persuaded the king to swear to keep the Provisions of Oxford (24). The Provisions of Oxford required a Grand Council of twenty-four men, twelve chosen by the King, twelve by the barons, to administer the country. Inevitably Henry followed King John's example and once again, the barons went to war. At the Battle of Lewes in 1264, the king was deposed by Simon de Montfort. He did not want the crown for himself, and so called another Great Council which he later called a Parliament. Hitherto, the assembly which had helped the king to govern England had consisted of barons and senior churchmen. However, not content with this, Simon called two knights from each shire and two citizens from each city. In effect, what we have here is the first House of Commons and the first seeds of democracy.

After a further bout of civil war culminating in a battle at Evesham in AD 1265, Simon de Montfort – who had hitherto ruled extremely well – was deposed by Prince Edward. Ironically, Prince Edward's first act was to summon the shire knights and citizens and, by doing so, established a principle that we govern by today. No Parliament is properly formed without representatives of the people. At that time the barons, clergymen, knights and citizens all met together in one chamber and they continued to do so for fifty years before separate chambers were established. This also established London as two cities: the King's City (Westminster) and the Merchants' City (The City of London).

Scotland

At this stage it might be appropriate to consider the early history of Scotland. Scotland, as we know it today, comprises a central plain between the Firth of Clyde and the Firth of Forth, where most of the population lives in two great cities – Glasgow and Edinburgh. Most of the agriculture takes place on this plain. To the south, there is a thinly populated area of moorland and upland and, to the north, is an even more thinly populated and mountainous region known as the Scottish Highlands. At the time of the Romans, the central plain and the Highlands were occupied by the Picts but, as the Romans left, migrants from the north east of Ireland (Ulster – now referred to as Northern Ireland), and whom the Romans had named "Scotiae", began to settle in north western England, north of the River Ribble in Lancashire and south western Scotland up to the River Clyde. This latter area is known as Strathclyde. The pictish inhabitants were driven north. The eastern part of southern and central Scotland had already been colonised by the Angles of Northumbria. The union of Scotland began under Kenneth MacAlpin who, in 843AD, united the Picts and the Scots in a single kingdom, called Alban. Then in 945AD, King Edmund of Wessex made peace with King Malcolm of Scotland and leased Strathclyde to him. Later, in 966, Edmund ceded the other side of the country, Lothian, to his successor, Kenneth 2nd. The process is sometimes described as the Scots subduing Lothian and the Angles of Lothian subduing the whole of Scotland. The border between England and Scotland was finally established in 1222AD. None of this was to bring prolonged peace between England and Scotland. Aside from relations between the two adjoining countries, it is worth mentioning at this point that Orkney and Shetland (25), the islands to the north of Scotland, were, at this time, part of the kingdom of Denmark. As part of the dowry of Princess Margaret of Denmark, on her marriage to King James 3rd of Scotland, the islands were passed to Scottish rule in 1469. The islanders still resent it and make much of their Norse heritage even today. It is noticeable today, that, whilst government and government agency buildings fly the Saltire of St. Andrew – a white, diagonal cross on a blue background – private buildings fly the respective flags of Orkney and of Shetland. The similarity in the style of these flags to those of the Scandinavian countries cannot be missed. Scotland's bid for independence from Great Britain may well have resurrected desires for independence among the islanders of Orkney and Shetland.

England again...

Having established an English parliament in a nation now united, Edward wanted to unite England and Wales. Over time, large parts of Wales had been subdued and now Edward wanted to complete the job but Llewellyn, the welsh ruler, refused to submit. So, Edward led an army into Wales and Llewellyn withdrew to the Snowdonia area (26), which is mountainous and rugged. Llewellyn's view was that the king would not follow him into an area that would be so disadvantageous to the English army. Edward, seeing what might have been a trap, simply blocked up the passes and blockaded the coast, then waited until Llewellyn's army were starved into submission. His submission was short-lived, however, and three years later he and his brother raised another army and rebelled. Llewellyn was killed in this conflict and his brother David captured, subsequently to be executed. Edward appointed his son – also Edward – as Prince of Wales, setting a precedent which is kept to this day: the oldest son of the monarch is still crowned as Prince of Wales. Prince Charles, oldest son of Queen Elizabeth 2nd and heir to the throne, is the present title holder. When Prince Charles eventually ascends to the throne, Prince William will be crowned Prince of Wales.

Back to Scotland

Edward now turned his attention to Scotland. Relations with Scotland had at this time been quite cordial. The King of Scotland, Alexander 3rd, had just died and the daughter of the King of Norway, Alexander's grand-daughter, Margaret, became heir to the Scottish crown. Edward proposed a marriage between his son and this young woman, known as the Maid of Norway. The result would have been to unite the crowns of Scotland and England and many in both England and Scotland agreed that it would be a good thing. Unfortunately, on the journey to Scotland, she became ill and had to be landed on the main island of Orkney, where she died. This left the Scottish crown with several claimants and a vacant crown: a recipe for civil war.

A meeting took place between Edward and the Scottish barons at which the question of succession was discussed. In the end, a man called John Balliol was placed on the throne and pledged obedience to King Edward. Balliol himself was not popular in many quarters of Scotland and a dispute with a Scottish baron proved to be the flashpoint. Edward decided to have the matter heard in England and put Balliol in an impossible position: if he obeyed, the Scots would dethrone him; if he disobeyed, King Edward would dethrone him. In the end, he disobeyed and Edward marched north to Berwick, where he sacked the town. He then marched further north to Dunbar, where he comprehensively defeated the Scots and took Scotland for himself. This triggered a change of heart amongst the Scottish barons.

If the Scots people disliked Balliol, they liked the idea of an English conquest even less and they were determined to resist. The Scottish barons at that time were of largely Norman descent and reasonably in sympathy with Edward. The people saw things differently and anti-English, independent sentiment soon found a leader in Sir William Wallace. After a brawl in Lanark, he had taken to the hills as an outlaw and soon found himself surrounded by a band of warriors determined to resist English incursions. In 1298, he met the English army at the bridge of the River Forth near Stirling and wiped out a third of it, mainly as a result of bad tactical decisions by the English commander. Flushed with success, Wallace then invaded England but then, hearing of approaching English retaliation, took his army into hiding. Wallace's hideout was betrayed, the King's army came upon Wallace's army at Falkirk (27) and defeated it comprehensively. Eventually, Wallace was again betrayed and handed over to the King Edward's sheriff, Sir John Mentieth, then taken to London for trial. He was hanged and his body cut into four pieces, which were then fixed to the gates of Berwick, Newcastle, Perth and Stirling – in other words, he was hung, drawn and quartered.

This did not, however, subdue the Scots, who found another leader in Robert Bruce, grandson of one of Balliol's rivals. More battles ensued, mostly to the advantage of the Scots, for Edward had died and his successor, Edward 2nd, was no army commander. He was finally deposed and Edward 3rd took up the battle. He decided that Scotland was unconquerable and made peace in 1328.

The Hundred Years' Wars

The struggle between England and France over the dominion of south-west France, is referred to as the Hundred Years War and it lasted from 1338 to 1453. England's claim was essentially based on a desire to regain the lands lost by King John a century earlier. It was not a continuous war. There were truces and intervals of peace, but the conflict continued sporadically.

The hundred years' war is remembered for three great battles, which the English won, spectacularly. There was a difference in their weaponry: the French used the crossbow, which was easier to use and had a good range, whereas the English armies used the longbow. The longbow needed more skill to use effectively but could achieve a much higher rate of fire – some 10-12 arrows per minute against 2 per minute from a crossbow – and, in practised hands the longbow was quite accurate and powerful. In modern infantry context, one might use the crossbow for sniping duties whereas the longbow would be used as an assault weapon. The battle victories of Crecy (26th August 1346), Poitiers (19th September 1356) and Agincourt (25th October 1415) had one characteristic in common: the English armies were heavily outnumbered (by 3.5:1 at Crecy by 6:1 at Poitiers and at Agincourt by 5:1) but the rate of fire achieved by the longbowmen, coupled with the power of arrows as they struck their targets, devastated the armies confronting them. The first rows of the French armies were cut down and their corpses impeded the progress of the ranks behind them, leaving them even more vulnerable to the rain of arrows.

Some of the longbowmen were under orders to bring down the horses of the French knights, leaving them to attack on foot as best they could, heavily encumbered by heavy armour. In each case, the French forces were almost wiped out.

These battles demonstrated the effectiveness of the longbow against the heavy armour of the mediaeval knights. Neither cavalry nor crossbowmen were able to fight against armies equipped with the longbow. Consequently, the tradition of knights with heavy armour was brought to an end.

Ironically, neither English supremacy nor armament won the war. The French did what many armies do when they are out-gunned. They stayed in their fortified cities while the English were around, knowing that they were safe but resorted to guerrilla tactics when they could do so safely. In the end, the French held on to the territories they had taken from King John.

The Black Death and the End of the Feudal System

The feudal system, which was an exploitative Norman version of the old Saxon manorial system, involved small farmers having to work certain days on the land of their landlord. It had worked reasonably well under the Saxon regime but had been regarded as oppressive since the Norman Conquest. The descendants of the Norman conquerors, who still despised their Saxon tenants, sought to exploit them to the maximum degree. However, as agriculture and agricultural markets developed, it became common for tenants to pay their lord instead of working. That worked reasonably well: the tenant could work full time on his own land and the landlord could hire labourers as and when he needed them.

The Black Death – an outbreak of what was probably bubonic plague – changed all that. It was endemic in parts of Asia. The spread of the disease began when a Turkic army, while besieging a Genoese trading post in Asia, catapulted corpses infected with the disease into the town. From there, it spread into Europe via ship-borne black rats and from the ports it spread inland. The filthy streets of mediaeval towns and cities were a perfect breeding ground for the fleas and mosquitoes which bit both rats and people, thus spreading the disease to the human population. The main outbreak in England took place from 1347 to 1350 and a second plague – the Children's Plague of 1361 – wiped out about a quarter of the children. There were two or three further outbreaks by 1400.

47

It killed nearly half the European population and in some cases, wiped out whole communities. Much of the European economy was devastated and the repercussions lasted for decades afterwards. One children's song survives from the time – Ring a Ring of Roses.

In rural areas, the shortage of manpower led to labourers demanding vastly higher wages and the stage was quickly reached where a man's wages exceeded by some margin the payment made by the tenant farmer in lieu of service. The shortage of manpower caused food shortages and starvation. Crops often could not be harvested and were left to rot in fields. Inevitably, this caused rampant inflation and Parliament tried to act by legislating to restrain prices and wages. Despite the harsh punishments entailed, the laws were widely ignored. Landlords then tried to reverse "commuting" arrangements and force tenant farmers to revert to service in the landlords' fields. This, too, was largely unsuccessful and caused much resentment.

This rumbling resentment erupted when, in 1380, parliament introduced a poll tax, which bore much more heavily on the poor than it did on the wealthy. This poll tax was introduced because –as another consequence of the aftermath of the Black Death – tax revenues had fallen and Parliament was desperate for money. The shortage of labour caused poverty among the landowning classes, who could not harvest and sell their farm produce, nor could they replace easily the tenants who had died, so they lost both payments of rent and farm revenues. That caused the King's revenues to fall. The end result of the poll tax was a trigger to a revolt by peasant farmers in East Anglia and southern England, led by, amongst others, Wat Tyler. This was the Peasants' Revolt of 1381. Tyler led a large group to London to protest and was met by King Richard 2nd and the Mayor of London at Smithfield (28). Fearing that the mob was about to attack the King, the Mayor killed Tyler and shortly afterwards the Peasants' Revolt was put down.

Then the landed class came up with another solution: they introduced lease-holding of their lands by tenant farmers, so that hiring labour became a matter for the tenant farmers. Even 30 years after the Black Death, the population had not recovered to its previous level and food shortages were still causing starvation but, at least, lease-holding largely blunted the anger of the tenants since, most importantly, they retained their independence. The cost of labour was still too high and land-holders were consequently attracted to reducing their dependence on arable farming – raising crops – to concentrate on producing wool. Wool was a much-in-demand fabric and raising sheep was an activity that could be supported by a couple of shepherds.

Thus, sheep farming meant rural employment changed very quickly from labour shortages to mass unemployment and landlords who had struggled to keep their workers now wanted to get rid of them. In many cases, common land was enclosed and tenant farmers' lands, which depended on the use of common land to supplement their own grazing land, ceased to be viable. Most left the countryside to find employment in the towns and tenant farmers –or serfs – disappeared from rural England. Thus it was the Black Death and its aftermath that brought an end to the feudal system.

One other important development took place at about this time, in the 1370s. That was the introduction of buttons and it drove radical changes in dress – especially for the better off – since it meant that clothing need no longer be pulled over the head or pulled up over the legs. It could be wrapped around and the buttons fastened, meaning that it could be closer fitting and, perhaps, more flattering in shape.

Religion

During the reign of King Edward 3rd, there was widespread dislike of the Pope's interference in English affairs and a great deal of resentment at the large sums of money sent to Rome as taxes. They also resented the way that the Pope appointed foreign churchmen, who then often held several livings without ever visiting any of them. These churchmen lived rather too well. Even the Friars, the Dominican and Franciscan orders, had gradually lost their devotion to poverty and simplicity and began to live like rich men. This contrasted with the poverty of parish priests and gave rise to the oft quoted axiom that "God gave his people to be pastured, not shaven and shorn" and the idea that some sort of reform was needed. This feeling was exacerbated by the move, in 1309, of the Pope from Rome to Avignon. The French were hated in England and the reputation of the upper echelons of the church was further damaged when, in 1378, two priests claimed the papacy: one in Rome and one in Avignon (29).

At that time, The Master of Balliol College, Oxford, a Yorkshireman named John Wycliff, became the primary critic of the church. He reasoned that the main faults of the church came from its pursuit of wealth and power on earth and he pointed out that nothing in the Bible justified the taxes paid to Rome, nor the holding of more than one living by senior churchmen. He founded a movement called the Simple Priests. His views gained popularity because, unlike the rest of scholars or churchmen, he wrote his tracts in English: thus by using the language of the people, he anticipated Martin Luther by about

100 years. He went further. He translated the Bible from Latin to English so that ordinary people – or at least, those who could read – could read the Bible for themselves. The movement – by then referred to as the Lollards – increased dramatically in numbers but, in the later years of Richard 3rd and later after Henry 4th came to the throne, the church retaliated against what they described as heresy and many Lollard "heretics" were burned at the stake. Thus Lollardry, which was never more than a one-issue campaign, declined and was eventually extinguished.

The Wars of the Roses

The Wars of the Roses were a dispute over succession to the English Crown. Edward 3rd's oldest son, the Black Prince, predeceased him but left a son who became Richard 2nd. Richard had no children either and was deposed by his cousin, Henry of Lancaster, who became Henry 4th. There were, however, other claimants who were descended from Edward 3rd and who represented the lines of Clarence and York. Clarence was an older line of descent than Lancaster and probably had a stronger claim to the throne. When a Clarence married a York, their child, Richard of York, was a strong and natural claimant to the throne.

Subsequently Richard of York raised an army and attempted to depose Henry 6th from the throne. Richard of York's hereditary claim notwithstanding, Parliament had accepted Henry and that choice had support throughout the country. Parliament considered that it had the right to appoint the king as it saw fit. Henry, however, was both a weak and an unlucky king and in his later years was thought to be mad. So, the idea spread that it would be better if a strong king were to succeed him and that meant Richard of York. Thus began some 40 years of civil war and turmoil.

After some five years of civil war, in 1461, Henry 6th was deposed and supplanted by Richard' successor, Edward 4th. The battles did not end there, and Henry managed at one point to regain his crown, but Edward fought back and eventually regained power. Edward's son, who inherited the crown, was deposed and murdered - at the tender age of 13 - by Richard of Gloucester who took the throne as Richard 3rd. Richard was deformed by scoliosis and was known as Crookback. He reigned for two years, after which he was killed in 1485 at the Battle of Bosworth (30) after a daring and incautious personal charge at the enemy. That victorious enemy was Henry Tudor, and he restored the Lancastrian line by being crowned Henry 7th. That said, his lineage gave him only a highly questionable claim to the throne – 9th or 10th in line – and his relationship to the House of Lancaster was distant. He was the grandson of Owen Tudor, a Welsh aristocrat and palace retainer who had married Catherine, the widow of Henry 5th. During this time, the whole country was in turmoil and there was virtually no law or order. Barons who had their own private armies made their own law and throughout the period, armies changed sides as they saw fit. Indeed, the Lancastrian victory at Bosworth was achieved because Sir William Stanley's (later to become Earl of Derby) army changed sides mid-battle to support the Lancastrians. Stanley's forces, having been on the side of the Yorkists, were able to hang back and then attack Richard and his army from behind. And there was brutality on both sides; prisoners being butchered was a regular occurrence. Small wonder, then, that animosity between the counties of Yorkshire and Lancashire continues to this day and even sporting contests are seen as a re-run of the Wars of the Roses.

When it was all over, there were few barons left and the people regarded the Tudors, for all their rather despotic style of rule and their status as usurpers, as the lesser of two evils compared to the conflict of the previous years. It is generally overlooked that the Tudors, who reigned from 1485 to 1603, were, in fact, Welsh monarchs.

In the autumn of 2012, excavations below a car park in Leicester revealed a body buried in what had been an ancient monastery. By the spring of the following year, it was established that the body was that of King Richard 3rd. We now know how he died – he was struck from behind by an arrow, then suffered an horrendous blow – again from behind – by an axe, probably a halberd, which was an axe and spear or pike, combined. That final, fatal blow sliced part of Richard's skull apart. That tallies with other information that the King was attacked from behind by Stanley's retainers. King Richard is reburied in Leicester Cathedral.

War of the Roses 1455 - 1487

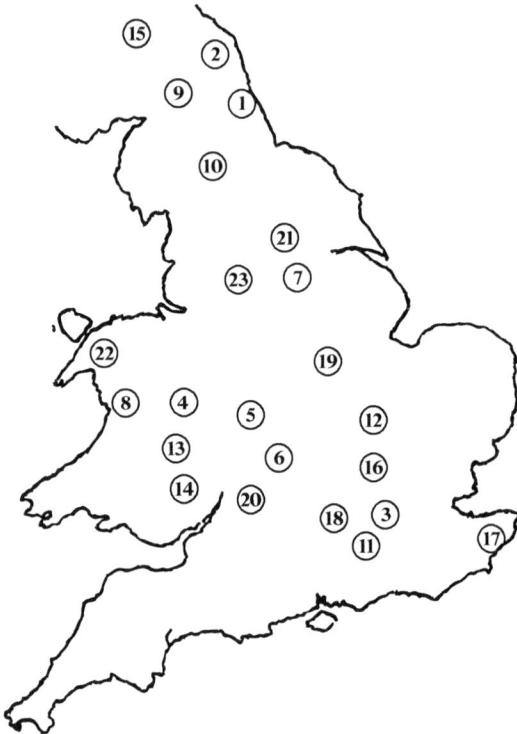

Key:

1. Alnwick (1462, 1463)	9. Hedgeley Moor (1464)	17. Sandwich (1460)
2. Bamburgh (1462, 1464)	10. Hexham (1464)	18. St. Albans (1455, 1461)
3. Barnet (1471)	11. London (1471)	19. Stoke (1487)
4. Blore Heath (1459)	12. Losecoat Field (1470)	20. Tewkesbury (1471)
5. Bosworth (1485)	13. Ludford Bridge (1459)	21. Towton (1461)
6. Edgecote Moor (1469)	14. Mortimers Cross (1461)	22. Twt Hill (1461)
7. Ferrybridge (1461)	15. Norham (1463)	23. Wakefield (1461)
8. Harlech (1468)	16. Northampton (1460)	

The Reformation and the Rise of Protestantism.

The new King, Henry 7th, spent much of his reign in what might today be described as mopping up operations, trying – not entirely successfully – to prevent any further outbreak of the wars. He forbade the keeping of uniformed retainers and taxed the barons so that he could retain a great hoard of money, which could be used to reinforce his position, politically, diplomatically or militarily, as circumstances might demand. He also gave his daughter Margaret for the wife of King James 4th of Scotland, which was to have repercussions later on and which continue to echo even to the present day.

Henry 7th died in 1509 and was succeeded by Henry 8th, who is probably better known for his six wives than for anything else that he did. Nevertheless, Henry 8th's legacy is significant in several ways. He had two great rivals to contend with: the King of France and the King of Spain, the latter of whom also ruled what is now Holland and Belgium, a large section of what is now Germany and part of Italy. It is they – and Henry's inability to father a son from his first and second marriages – who were the main factors in the most momentous consequences of Henry's reign: the break from Rome. Henry wanted to divorce Queen Catherine of Aragon, cousin of the King of Spain. His application to the Pope should have been a routine matter but Pope Clement feared the King of Spain – who had large armies all over much of Italy – more than he

BRITISH HISTORY IN BRIEF

feared Henry, so he refused the divorce. In his fury, Henry disgraced his envoy, Cardinal Wolsey, and decided to break with Rome.

Something of a precedent had been set by a priest from Eisleben in Saxony, Martin Luther, who sparked off the reformation in the princedoms of the Holy Roman Empire (now Germany), and who, in 1517, had protested over the misbehaviour of many senior churchmen. He had encouraged his flock to take their beliefs from the Bible rather than from Rome, and eventually established the Protestant Church. Henry Tudor did not want actually to change his beliefs or his religious practices, nor did Parliament. So, his Act of Supremacy in 1529, made the King the head of the church but there were no religious changes. Strictly, then, Henry was neither catholic nor protestant but had cut off Rome from appeals, from payments and so on. He then required all churchmen to swear the Oath of Supremacy and those who refused were either beheaded or burnt at the stake. One of the last vestiges of papal authority was among the monasteries, so in 1535, Henry dissolved the smaller monasteries and, seeing how much wealth was there for the taking, dissolved the major monasteries four years later. He then authorised another translation of the Bible from Latin into English and allowed these to be kept in churches. The translation work was carried out by a man named Miles Coverdale. Printing had replaced hand-copying, which resulted in Bibles becoming much cheaper to produce, so Henry allowed people to have Bibles in their homes. Of course, there was still a large section of the population who could not read, but literacy had spread from the churches to the nobility and middle classes.

Henry 8th's main concern was to produce a son and heir. His first wife, Catherine of Aragon, produced only a daughter Mary, and in 1531, Henry had the marriage annulled. He then, on 23rd May 1533, married Anne Boleyn, who produced another daughter –Elizabeth. Despairing of her ability to give him a son, he had her executed on questionable charges of adultery and incest on 19th May 1536. Eleven days later, he married his next wife, Jane Seymour, who gave him a son, Edward, but she died a few days later on 24th October 1537. Death in or shortly after childbirth was not unusual at the time. His next wife was Anne of Cleves, whom he found singularly unattractive and it is possible that the marriage was never consummated. He married Anne on 6th January 1540 and divorced her on 9th July of that year. On 28th July, he married Catherine Howard, but she produced nothing, so he had her executed on 25th November 1541. Finally, he married Catherine Parr on 12th July 1543. Despite not producing any children, she survived and remained queen until Henry himself died in 1547.

Two years earlier, 1545, during a confrontation with France, Henry had watched a sea battle from the shore at Portsmouth. The French navy was driven off but Henry's flagship, the formidably-armed Mary Rose, heeled over and sank, probably because of instability arising from its complement of cannon. In 1982, the wreck of the Mary Rose was raised from the sea-bed and was placed in a preserving museum at Portsmouth Dockyard. The wreck-site has now been more thoroughly excavated and explored and now the remains of the Mary Rose and the artefacts found around the wreck have been placed in a new museum, opened in 2012 in the dockyard at Portsmouth, allowing visitors to see the remains more clearly and to examine the huge haul of artefacts associated with the ship.

When Henry 8th died, he left three legitimate children: Mary, daughter of his first wife, Queen Catherine of Aragon; Elizabeth, daughter of his second wife, Anne Boleyn; and Edward, son of his third wife, Jane Seymour.

Edward was only 9 years old when he ascended to the throne and was placed under the direction of a regent, the Duke of Somerset. Somerset took the reformation much further than Henry had done but made himself very unpopular, particularly in rural areas. Indeed, there were rebellions in Devonshire and Norfolk, which proved difficult to put down.

Somerset was replaced by the self-interested Duke of Northumberland who made things even worse. He married his own son to Lady Jane Grey (who had a claim to the throne) and when Edward died in 1553, tried to put Jane

Grey on the throne. That lasted nine days – hence Jane Grey's epithet as the nine-days queen – at which point she was beheaded, along with her husband. She was replaced by Queen Mary, the half-Spanish older daughter of Henry 8th. Being catholic – and married to the King Philip of Spain – she naturally proceeded to reintroduce Catholicism to the country and burnt at the stake many of those who demurred. In all, she burnt some 300 dissenters, including a number of bishops.

Mary died in 1558 and was succeeded by Queen Elizabeth 1st, the red-haired daughter of Henry and Anne Boleyn. This was a relief to the English, if only because Elizabeth was protestant. Indeed, a protestant disinclined to worry about just what people believed, provided they went to church and acknowledged her as head of the English church. Elizabeth had many proposals of marriage but was unable to accept any of them: it enabled her, while she was "available" for marriage, to play diplomatic games which neither a king nor a married queen would be able to. Indeed, there was only one small movement of opposition to her, religiously, namely a small clique which believed that it was wrong for her to be head of the church. Indeed, they did not accept that the church needed an earthly head. This clique was to grow in number and in influence later on. They were known as the Puritans.

Elizabeth's ascent to the English throne was not to the advantage of King Philip of Spain. While he had been married, albeit briefly, to her half-sister, Queen Mary, not only was England kept safely catholic but he could maintain a garrison in the Netherlands – loosely, modern day Holland and Belgium – and restrain the protestant inclinations of the Netherlanders. This was important to Philip, because he was related to the Habsburgs, the ruling family of the Austrian empire, and that gave him the necessary status to be eligible for election as emperor of the Holy Roman Empire. At that time, The Holy Roman Empire, now known as Germany, was multiplicity of principalities, dukedoms and bishoprics whose rulers elected an emperor who ruled for life. He now had a monarch on the English throne who actively encouraged the resistance among Netherlands protestants and hindered the Inquisition, whose task it was to seek out protestants and convert or burn them. He decided to invade and, in 1586/7, began to put together a fleet of ships – the Spanish Armada. He was happy for this to become known in England, hoping that it would intimidate the English and their Queen. It did no such thing. It merely provoked Sir Francis Drake to attack the fleet in Cadiz harbour (31) and set fire to several ships: "singeing the king of Spain's beard" he called it. Drake was hated by the Spanish: they thought him little more than a pirate. He had deprived Spain of a great deal of its wealth by attacking and – after confiscating their cargoes – sinking many of its silver bullion ships as they left the Caribbean. It was thought, probably correctly, that he had the blessing of the English Queen.

The Armada sailed for England in July 1588. The plan was to collect soldiers from Holland then invade England, depose Elizabeth and return the country to Catholicism. As the Armada sailed up the English Channel, the news was sent to London by a series of beacons lit on hilltops. The Armada was attacked in the Channel by Drake, whose fleet had been in harbour at Plymouth (32). The tradition of Drake finishing a game of bowls before setting sail may or may not be true, but a likely factor is that he had to await the tide. Initially, little damage was sustained by the Armada but they did use a great deal of ammunition. Then the Armada commander discovered that, because of the draught of the ships, he would have to heave to just off Calais (33) and await the Netherland garrison. That made the Armada vulnerable because they had to break formation. The English fleet attacked again, this time with fire-ships – old, time-served craft filled with inflammable materials, set on fire and released upstream of the tide so that they drifted toward the Armada. This did do substantial damage and caused the commander to abandon the invasion of England. This, however, presented the Armada command with a dilemma: the ships could not retreat through the English Channel, which was blocked by the English fleet. The inevitable decision was therefore made, to retreat via the north coast of Scotland. This was probably the only choice open but what was left of the Armada ran into an horrendous storm. Consequently, many of the Spanish ships were wrecked. Things got worse: the survivors hoped to be able to put in at Galway (34), on the west coast of catholic Ireland and to reprovision, only to find themselves attacked again and sailors killed. The Irish regarded Spain as an enemy and treated both sailors and ships accordingly. The experience put paid to any further Spanish ambitions to invade this country.

Part of Queen Elizabeth's legacy is the introduction of tobacco, which reached Europe in 1571. So popular was it that a Spanish doctor "established tobacco as a cure for some twenty ailments" – of which one was cancer.

The other part of her legacy is dramatic, for it was during this period that William Shakespeare wrote most of his plays. The son of an affluent tanner, William was born in Stratford upon Avon, Warwickshire, in April 1564 and married Anne Hathaway in 1582. At the time, he was 18 and she 26 – and pregnant. Their first child, Susanna was born in May 1583 and the twins Hamnet and Judith born in 1585. By 1590, he was a managing partner in the Lord Chamberlain's Actors and it was during this time that he wrote many of his historical plays, a list of which is in the appendix. At first he used a number of venues around London but in 1598, work started on a dedicated theatre – The Globe – and Shakespeare plays were presented from 1598 until 1642, when the Puritan regime closed it down. Of course, since he did not want to lose his head at the Tower of London, he had to be aware of the political atmosphere, since Queen Elizabeth could be both capricious and precipitate. The situation did not become any easier even after 1603, when King James ascended to the throne. Shakespeare died in April 1616.

The Stuarts

Elizabeth 1st died in 1603: the heir next in line to the throne was a scot, James Stuart, who became James 1st of England and 6th of Scotland. This was a consequence of the marriage of Margaret, Henry 7th's daughter, to James 4th, King of Scotland.

The result was that for the first time, the crowns of England and Scotland were united, though they remained separate countries. James was much taken with the wealth to which he now had access in contrast to the comparative poverty of the Scottish kings. He became profligate: in 1605, out of his grant of £460,000, given to run the state, its palaces and the royal households, King James gave away £41,500 to three Scottish friends who had run up huge gambling debts. He compounded this by spending £8000 on "spangle" for his guards. His drinking habits did not endear him either, for he was regularly and spectacularly drunk after drinking sessions with his brother-in-law.

Like his predecessor, Queen Elizabeth, James was, provided he was recognised as the Head of the Church in England and Scotland, disinclined to concern himself with exactly how people worshipped. That was not acceptable to some Catholics who were aware that James' daughter, another Elizabeth, was being brought up by her mother as a Catholic. They thought up a wild scheme to usurp the throne, get rid of the king and place Elizabeth on the throne. Robert Catesby, Sir Everard Digby, Thomas Percy, Robert and Thomas Wintour,

Thomas Bates, Robert Keyes, Francis Tresham, and Ambrose Rookwood, the ring leaders of the plot, recruited a mercenary and explosives specialist, Guy Fawkes, to blow up the Houses of Parliament. They rented a cellar under Parliament and began assembling a destructive charge of gunpowder. In fact, by the time they were ready – they planned to strike at the opening of Parliament on 5th November 1605 – they had enough gunpowder to destroy much of Westminster, including the Abbey and the surrounding buildings. The secret leaked out, the cellars were searched, and Fawkes was discovered with his explosives. The plot was put down and the ring leaders executed. For Catholics in general, most of whom were perfectly loyal subjects, the result was disastrous: for many years afterwards, all Catholics were regarded and treated as traitors.

King James then managed to antagonise the Puritans. Religiously, they believed in the utmost simplicity. They did not like grand ceremonies in church, or the giving of wedding rings on marriage or the giving of the sign of the cross in baptism. And they did not approve of bishops. The king, inept as ever and egged on by the bishops, took a hard line with the Puritans, claiming that he ruled by divine right. From this arose the King's mantra "no bishop, no king". This further antagonised his Scottish subjects who, likewise, did not like bishops. In fact, Scottish bishops were widely ignored and disobeyed and were effectively powerless. The King's foreign policy made things worse, even though he was trying to be a peacemaker. He made diplomatic overtures to Spain – probably the country most hated by his English and Scottish subjects. Less than 20 years after the attempted invasion and the destruction of the Armada, the country at large was more interested in war with Spain than with peace overtures.

One interesting but largely forgotten series of event took place in America. Contact between settlers and native Indians, who regarded the settlers as trespassers, was fractious. In 1610, in what is now Virginia, the settlement of Jamestown greeted one John Rolfe, a tobacco grower. He met Mataoka, better known by her nickname, Pocohontas, who had been taken hostage by Captain Samuel Argall, in the hope of using her to negotiate peace with the local Powhatoan tribe. She was treated well in her captivity and not only learned English but converted to Christianity. Rather than accept her release in 1614, she decided to marry John Rolfe. Their first child, Thomas, was born in 1615. In 1616, they travelled to England and were presented to the court of King James. In March 1617, they prepared to return to Virginia, but the day before they sailed, Pocohontas died. She was buried in the church of St George, Gravesend, Kent. Rolfe returned to Virginia alone but was killed in a massacre in 1622. After being educated in England, his son Thomas Rolfe returned to Virginia and became a prominent citizen. Pocohontas' grave is not now identifiable, but her statue is placed in where her grave is thought to be, in St George's Church graveyard.

King James' son, Charles, married Henrietta Maria, sister to the King of France – and she was a Catholic. This was not, of course, a love match but a diplomatic, political and dynastic one and it was widely feared that his father James was a closet Catholic – which he was. England expected Henrietta to convert her husband to Catholicism which, in turn, meant the likelihood that after James' death, Charles would impose it on the country. James 1st lost the trust of both the English and the Scots. For example, James' daughter Elizabeth married Frederick the Elector Palatine – a staunch protestant and a German – but the gesture misfired because he was turned out of his realm by the Spaniards. James was unable to recover the realm for him either by diplomacy or by warfare. Then, in 1625, Charles ascended to the throne and inherited the suspicion of his subjects along with the crown. He sent a fleet to assist the French protestants at La Rochelle (35) but this was beaten off and the country saw it as an empty gesture, intended to reassure the public that his Catholic wife had not converted him.

Both kings were constantly at loggerheads with Parliament. Both believed that they were anointed by God and that opposition to them in any circumstances was sinful. Charles was particularly strong in his belief – despite the constitution which stated that parliament had the sole right to grant money and much else – that it was beneath the dignity of a king to defer in any way to Parliament. It would be contrary to what they regarded as Royal Prerogative. Both kings tried at times to override parliament. In 1628, Charles tried to bypass parliament in the raising of taxes but was subsequently forced to sign the Petition of Right, which reinforced parliament's supremacy in the raising and spending of taxes and, just as important, that the king could not command imprisonment without trial. This reinforced two very important clauses in the Magna Carta.

At that time, ministers were nevertheless appointed by the king. Even today, whilst ministers are appointed and dismissed by the Prime Minister, they are nevertheless referred to as Ministers of the Crown. However, the Earl of Middlesex was impeached for misusing public money as was the Duke of Buckingham, for failing in the war against Spain. Impeachment was a system under which the House of Commons accused a man and he would be brought before the House of Lords for judgement. In the affairs of the King, this was unprecedented interference by Parliament. In his first four years on the throne, Charles quarrelled with Parliament three times. On each occasion, he dissolved parliament but then quarrelled with the next. Eventually, Charles decided to rule without parliament and he did so for eleven years – the Eleven Years of Tyranny (1629-1640.) Charles then tried to get the Irish parliament to vote him money and he also tried to revive Ship Money. Ship Money was a tax imposed on coastal counties to raise money for wartime naval activities. Charles, however, imposed it in peacetime, illegally, and on inland counties.

A squire named John Hampden refused payment of Ship Money on the grounds that it was illegal and was tried before a Star Chamber court, which, fearing the wrath of the King if they dismissed the case, convicted Hamden and imposed a heavy fine. A Star Chamber court was, in effect, a king's court, which heard cases without a jury and often in secrecy, in the Palace of Westminster. It was a court system introduced by Henry 8th to circumvent those courts that had been riddled by corruption. Henry had used the courts sparingly and with great care: Charles was using it merely to impose unpopular political and religious policies, with those "convicted" often subjected to cruel or excessive punishments. The Star Chambers quickly became an instrument of oppression throughout the Years of Tyranny.

The Civil War and its Causes

Inept and arrogant as ever, King Charles 1st managed to antagonise even his subjects in Scotland. This time, it was over a religious service book he tried to introduce which was completely contrary to the tradition of the Presbyterian Church in Scotland. After an incident at a church in Edinburgh in which a chair was thrown at the priest, a resistance movement was organised by groups who called themselves "Tables". Charles' problem was that whilst Scotland (of which he was also king and a Scottish King to boot) had an effective army, he, in England, did not. In 1639, the Scottish army marched south as far as Yorkshire and the King had to sue for peace. This conflict is called the Bishops' War.

Charles, still very much his own worst enemy and completely untrustworthy, called a new Parliament. It became known as the Short Parliament because shortly after it assembled, the King quarrelled with it and dissolved it. He then called another Parliament which outlasted him – 19 years, in fact, and known as the Long Parliament.

Pym, Hampden and their allies pressed on with their programme of reforms, curtailing the King's ability to act without Parliament and requiring him to rule according to law. They also decided to move against the King's Chief Minister, Lord Strafford, for allegedly inciting the King to use Irish troops to force his will on the English Parliament. This was a questionable charge, but Strafford was nevertheless executed. This really did restrict the King and he promised in future to act according to law.

Most Parliamentarians thought they had done enough and were quite happy to let matters rest as they were but, devious and inept as ever, the King retaliated by leading a number of troops – fully armed – to the House of Commons in order to arrest Hampden, Pym and three others. But, inevitably, forewarning of the plan had leaked out to those involved and they had left the House. This was a decisive moment: the whole House now knew that the King could not be trusted, that his promises could not be accepted as genuine and the whole issue could be settled only by warfare. So began the Civil War.

At first, the King's troops, led by Prince Rupert, had the upper hand. However, after some retreats, the King's troops were put on the defensive. An alliance between Parliament and Scotland brought Scottish troops to the Battle of Marston Moor but, in the event, they did very little. The star of the battle was an officer called Oliver Cromwell, who had raised his own regiment, which he had drilled and trained, convinced that training, discipline and morale – a New Model Army – made for a much more effective force than dash and loyalty. In the event, the King was soundly and utterly beaten.

Cromwell's regiment became known as the Ironsides, a reference to the steel armour they wore. The King's forces became known as the Cavaliers because, in the early stages of the war, they had markedly more cavalry. Cromwell had gathered good men around him because he was religiously independent: he wanted everyone to be able to worship as they pleased. That made him acceptable to a wide range of people and the enemy only of the King's army. In 1645, The New Model Army met the King's army at Naseby (35) and defeated them decisively. For the King, only Scotland remained as a last chance to retain power. However, a formidable army with a formidable leader – Montrose – was routed at Philiphaugh, not far from Berwick (37). King Charles, still devious, surrendered to the Scots at Newark (38), who – trusting him less than the English – promptly handed him over to Parliament in return for a promise to discharge the arrears of pay. Charles tried to play off the Scots against the Ironsides and there was a second civil war with a rising of Royalists in the south of England. This, too, was defeated by the Ironsides and it led the Ironsides to the conclusion that there would be no peace while the King was alive.

It was Cromwell and the Army who decided to execute the King and carried it out by having him beheaded in 1649. Parliament itself would not agree to the trial and execution of a king. Indeed, to some, the King became a martyr and England became, in effect, a military dictatorship. Charles' death did not bring much peace: both Scotland and Ireland recognised Charles' son as the heir to the throne and rebellion continued. The situation became more complicated because Parliament abolished the office of the king and set up a commonwealth instead.

Ireland was the first to rebel and Cromwell went there with his Ironsides. Irish troops held the town of Drogheda (39) against Cromwell who stormed the town and – with Cromwell's orders to show no mercy – massacred the defenders. The late King's army officers were driven out of the country and the population at large terrified by Cromwell's brutality. Even today, Irishmen refer to the "Black Curse of Cromwell". There was virtually no further resistance and the Irish Parliament was abolished, but its members were sent to serve in the Houses of Parliament in London.

Then, Scotland tried to negotiate with Charles 2nd, the dead King's son. There were two groups and, like his father, Charles tried to play off one against the other. Montrose tried to raise an army but it was comprehensively defeated. That left the second group, the Covenantors, and in 1650, their army faced Cromwell's Ironsides at Dunbar (40). The Covenantors gained an advantage by advancing, then retreating while operating a scorched earth tactic. Later, they made a tactical mistake by attacking at the wrong moment and Cromwell's army was able virtually to destroy the Scottish army. Cromwell nevertheless pursued the Scots northwards and Charles 2nd, seeing an opportunity, marched south, pursued by Cromwell. The two sides met at Worcester and it resulted in a resounding victory for Cromwell. So, now the whole country, England, Scotland, Ireland were conquered by Cromwell and now he wanted to subdue Parliament. He did this by leading troops into the House and expelling the Members.

Parliaments came and went under Cromwell, none of them successful. Having expelled a legitimate Parliament, he could not make his puppet Parliaments work. From then on, Cromwell operated pretty much as a military dictator until he died in 1659. On his death, rule passed to his son, Richard Cromwell but he, not being a military man, lasted only a year.

Thereafter, Charles 2nd returned. Charles was more sensible than his father and grandfather and was anxious not to get himself embroiled in arguments with Parliament. That said, having called a parliament and found that he could work with it, he kept it sitting for 18 years, yet he was still haunted by misfortune. Three great disasters happened on his watch.

The first, in 1665, was the outbreak of the Great Plague and, as with the Black Death 300 years earlier – it was another outbreak of bubonic plague – it made a huge impact on the population. Indeed, whole streets were closed, the houses boarded up and the dead were buried en-masse in plague pits dug outside the city boundaries. The houses of victims were marked by a red cross on the door and undertakers toured the streets, ringing bells and calling "Bring out your dead". Today, many of London's squares – and those of other towns and cities – came into being as the urban area expanded around these plague pits. The pits themselves cannot be opened up even today, for fear of releasing the infection. So, the developers of the day planted gardens over them and then built houses around them. It is important to note that plagues as such were not unusual: hygiene and sanitation had yet to be introduced and the streets in towns and cities were pretty filthy. The Black Death and the Great Plague are noteworthy only by virtue of severity and consequent death toll.

Then another disaster struck the following year, 1666. A fire in the City of London broke out in a bakery in Pudding Lane (London EC3) and spread rapidly, fanned by a wind from the south-east. It destroyed some ninety churches, including St Paul's Cathedral and thirteen thousand houses. To contain the fire, soldiers blew up houses in its path, to create a fire break. It finally ended having burned some two thirds of the city. Subsequently, the King had a monument (41) erected to commemorate the fire. It shows the King raising London in the form of a fallen woman, which attracted much ribald comment. The monument can be found near Monument underground station. It is a mistake to conclude that the Great Fire cleared out the plague. The plague centred mainly in what were known as the "freebies", in effect a shanty town to the east of the city. The Great Fire progressed westwards and burned out the more affluent areas of the city, where the plague had had rather less impact.

Charles' ill-fortune continued, for no sooner was the Great Fire extinguished but gunfire was heard in the Thames. Charles had neglected the navy, and the Dutch navy had sailed up the Thames, attacked the naval base at Chatham (Kent)(42) and might readily have attacked London but, fortunately, their courage failed and they sailed downstream and out into the sea.

The one useful change that emerged from Charles' reign was the Statute of Frauds, which introduced the use of a signature as means of validating documents, rather than the wax seals that had been used beforehand. Some legal documents still required a seal, but normal, everyday documents did not.

Charles then compounded his bad luck with stupidity. His grandfather had been a closet-Catholic, his father an overt one. Charles 2nd was, similarly, a discreet one but could not resist the temptation to make another attempt to force Catholicism on a protestant country. This brought the country to the brink of another civil war but fortunately this was avoided.

Main Battles of the English Civil War

Key:

1. Marston Moor (1645)
2. Naseby (1644)
3. Roundway Down (1643)
4. Newbury (1643)
5. Edgehill (1642)

Charles died in 1685 and was succeeded by his brother, James 2nd, an overt catholic. Headstrong and despotic, he intended to impose Catholicism on the country regardless. So soon after the controversy caused by Charles, this was a disastrous decision and it provoked a rebellion by his illegitimate half-brother, the Duke of Monmouth. The rebellion was put down easily and the King wreaked particularly brutal reprisals on the ringleaders. Encouraged by this success, he then began to force his religion on the church, which caused seven bishops to refuse to comply. They were tried but acquitted; this was the beginning of the end for James.

The Bloodless or Glorious Revolution

The one redeeming feature of King James 2nd was that his daughter and heiress, Mary, was Protestant and had married William of Orange. William was invited to England to take over the throne, which he did. On William's arrival, James' courtiers and supporters deserted him and James himself was taken prisoner. William sent him into exile in France and became King William 3rd, ruling jointly with Mary.

Nevertheless, Parliament required the new monarch to agree to a Bill of Right, which was ratified in 1688 (Julian Calendar: modern calendar – February 1689). This guaranteed the Rule of Law and the basic rights of the citizen. It still serves as a reference document for constitutional matters and takes precedence over any legislation passed by Parliament today, unless that Act of Parliament is enacted expressly as a constitutional Act. The Bill of Right can be seen in the Parliamentary Archive.

Scotland

The Bloodless revolution caused factions to emerge in Scotland. Some supported James 2nd, others, William. The battles in Scotland at this time are sometimes portrayed as conflicts between the King of England and the Scots. In fact, they were battles between Scottish factions, one supporting one side, one, the other. This was the case at the Pass of Killiecrankie (43), where in 1689 Viscount Dundee – a James supporter(Jacobite) – defeated MacKay, a King William supporter. This was followed by the Massacre of Glencoe, in which the William-supporting Campbell clan billeted themselves on the Jacobite McDonalds in Glencoe (44), then massacred them while they slept. There were further conflicts, loosely referred to as the Jacobite rebellion, which were driven by the fact that the Clan Campbell supported King William.

There were further Jacobite rebellions in Ireland too but, primarily, this was aimed at restoring a Catholic King. The early battles were between the Scottish Presbyterian forces and the Irish Catholic population but King William sent his own troops to rescue the Scottish Presbyterians at the Siege of Londonderry (45) in 1689 and put down a further rebellion led by King James himself at the Battle of the Boyne in 1690. The last battle was at Limerick (46) in 1691, after which James retreated to France after signing the Treaty of Limerick, which recognised William as King. All would have been well but the Irish Parliament insisted on persecuting Catholics, which exacerbated the hostility towards the English and the English Crown that continues to this day.

William proved a level-headed and tolerant king and, with the final overthrow of King James, came to agreement with Parliament. The formal agreement was the Bill of Right which prohibited the King from repealing or ignoring laws, keeping a standing army (this still applies: permission to maintain the armed forces still relies on annual renewal of the Army Act) in time of peace. It also provided that parliament had to be elected by free election, that Parliament could debate anything it chose to and, finally, that no King could be a catholic. So, from this moment on, Parliament became supreme. Initially, the King appointed ministers from both the main parties (Whig and Tory parties – loosely the present day Liberal Democrat Party and the Conservative Party) but it quickly arose that ministers based their power on whichever party had the majority of supporters. What we now had was the first – if imperfect – version of the modern party system.

Jacobite Rebellion - Main Battle Sites

Culloden Moor 1746
Inverness

Fort William

Glencoe 1689

Killiecrankie 1689

Dundee

Perth

Sheriffmuir 1715

Stirling

Prestonpans 1745

Edinburgh

Stonehenge

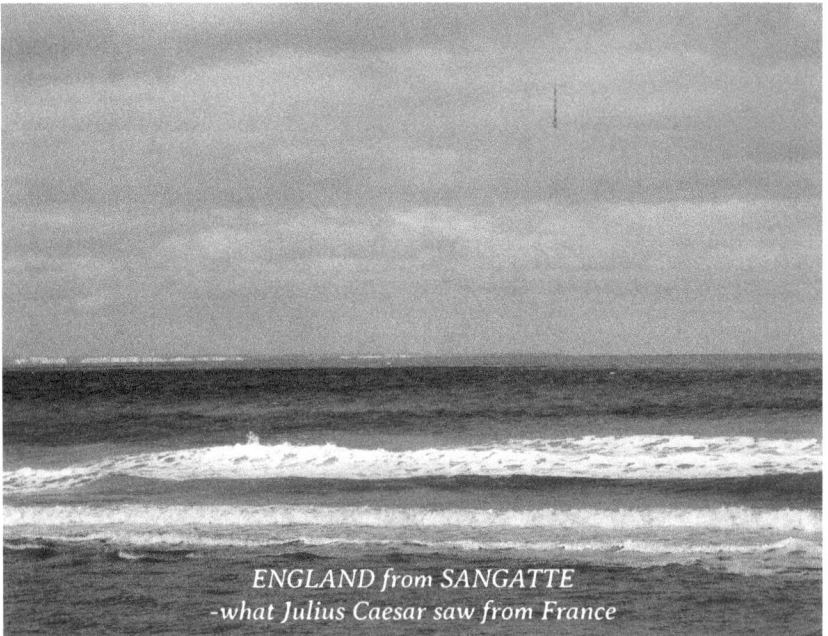

ENGLAND from SANGATTE
-what Julius Caesar saw from France

Hadrian's Wall

London Wall

Ironbridge

Tour bus – Waterloo

Waterloo Battle Memorial

Visitor centre – Waterloo Village Belgium

Site of Constable's Haywain nr Flatford Mill

Battle of Bosworth Memorial

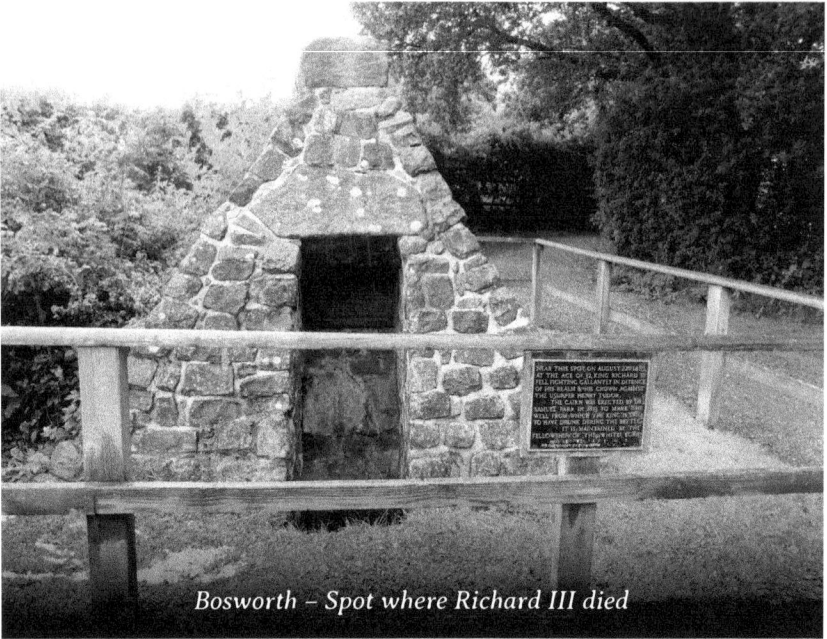

Bosworth – Spot where Richard III died

Arlington Row – 600 years old Bibury Cottages still lived in

The Second Hundred Years' War 1689-1815

William's accession to the throne coincided with the start of another war with France which lasted eight years. In fact, England was at war with France for over sixty of the next hundred and twenty-six years, ending with the Battle of Waterloo in 1815. Essentially, much of this conflict was driven by the quest for colonial power, although at times, the conflict between Catholicism and Protestantism served as a pretext. William was not terribly successful, but his defeats did not advance the French cause much, if at all.

One consequence of this war was the Window Tax (1696), which was levied on all windows according to their size. As a guide, this levied at two shillings (10p) for a small house to eight shillings (40p) for a large house. It was a much resented tax, variously described as daylight robbery, a tax on health and a tax on light and air. It was a hated tax, but it survived until its repeal in 1851.

William and Mary were succeeded in 1702 by Queen Anne who was fortunate to have John Churchill, Duke of Marlborough, as her army commander. He won battles: he had a very good appreciation of strategy and his victory at the Battle of Blenheim (47) in 1704 punctured what was seen as French invincibility. He went on to win further battles at Ramillies, Oudenaade and Malplaquet (48). These victories ended with the treaty of Utrecht of 1713, in which Britain gained Gibraltar, Minorca, Nova Scotia and St Kitts, the last being an important

BRITISH HISTORY IN BRIEF

centre for the slave trade. And it brought great wealth to Britain. Marlborough was rewarded with funds to build himself a grand house: Blenheim Palace at Woodstock, Oxfordshire (48), which is now open to the public. The palace is still lived in by the present Duke of Marlborough and the Churchill family. It is the birthplace of our 2nd World War hero, Sir Winston Churchill, who is a descendant of the family.

Scotland and the Union

Since the accession to the throne of James 1st, England and Scotland, whilst remaining separate countries, were ruled by the same monarch. The Scots were happy about this while the Stuarts reigned, and they accepted William because he ruled jointly with Queen Mary who was a Stuart. They were less keen when Queen Ann ascended to the throne: she was not Scottish, even though she carried Stuart blood. At the beginning of her reign, it was a distinct possibility that the Scots would want to break away and re-establish their own monarchy. What changed all that was the Darian Scheme.

The Darian Scheme, brainchild of a Scotsman called William Paterson, was a plan to establish a colony and a trading company in Darian (48), which we now know as Panama. He painted a picture of a fertile territory where agriculture could flourish and, being on a narrow isthmus between the Atlantic and Pacific Oceans, would be in a strategic position for trade. The idea was that cargoes for the Far East could be shipped to Darian, transferred to wagons and carried to the other side, then re-loaded onto ships on the Pacific coast. It would be a veritable paradise. In 1698, the would-be colonists set out from Scotland to the new country. Once there, they were attacked by the Spanish, found the territory ridden by disease and the climate unbearable. Only a few of the colonists lived to return and they were ruined by the failure of the project. It is recorded that almost half the wealth of Scotland had been invested in the Darian Scheme and the country faced bankruptcy.

Ann, faced with anger and the prospect of a bankruptcy in Scotland, proposed a union, in exchange for which the English treasury would make a grant to Scotland to pay off the national debt, i.e. to bail out the Scottish banks. The terms of the union were that Scotland and England were to form one realm, with Scottish members elected and admitted to the English Parliament but that Scottish law and the Scottish Presbyterian church should remain intact. So, on 1st May 1707, the Union of Scotland with England took place. Scotland was saved from penury, and prospered. The union was a success for some time afterwards.

Anne died in 1714. The Scots had been happy about rule from England for as long as there was a Stuart king on the throne. Ann had been accepted reluctantly but George 1st was of the House of Hanover and was so foreign that he spoke little English. The unhappy Jacobites began plotting again. An attempt to raise troops among the highland clans by the Earl of Mar was not terribly successful and, after one defeat, went on to meet the king's forces at Sheriffmuir (51). The battle was a draw and James 3rd – now known as the Old Pretender – arrived just afterwards. By that time, the rebellion was petering out with a whimper and James simply left the country.

Nothing more happened for thirty years, by which time, George 2nd had ascended to the throne. George was as German as his father but spoke better English. He was also at war with Spain and France. The son of James 3rd, Charles Edward, known, inevitably, as the Young Pretender, decided to try again. He had more luck. He routed the King's forces at Prestonpans (52) but was, himself, soundly defeated in 1746 at the Battle of Culloden Moor (53). Immediately after the battle, the young Pretender, also known as Bonnie Prince Charlie, was smuggled, with the help of Flora McDonald, westward to the Isle of Skye and shortly afterwards, back to France. This is the origin of the Skye Boat song, although in spite of the lyrics reference to "over the sea" and sea storms, the crossing is, in fact, relatively sheltered and the two primary crossing points (Kyle of Lochalsh to Kyleakin – now by bridge – and Glenelg to Kylerhea) are each just over a mile across. The song was written in 1884.

In the aftermath of the 1745 rebellion, King George 2nd conceived a master-stroke: he placed severe restrictions on the highland clans but raised among their young manhood, armies which he sent to fight his wars. That proved a sufficient distraction to pacify Scotland.

The Calendar Act

Since Roman times, the days and dates followed the calendar set by Julius Caesar. Loosely, the year began on 25th March (known as Lady Day) and the year was divided into quarter days: Lady Day, Midsummer's day (24th June), Michaelmas Day (29th September) and Christmas Day (25th December). In 1751, Parliament passed the Calendar Act, and shortened 1751, which ended on 31st December, after 280 days. The day after 31st December became the 1st January 1752 and that year lasted until 31st December 1752. Government still operates on something akin to the old Julian calendar: the tax year and civil service year still operates from 5th April to 4th April the next year.

The Advent of the Empire

Wars were a normal part of life for much of the 18th century, particularly the mid-century. In part, this was a result of King George's being king of Hanover with all its alliances. This dragged Britain into wars which, otherwise, would not have concerned it. In part, however, it was rivalry over colonial spoils. France, Spain, Holland and the Germanic States were all vying with each other for colonial territory. Germany as a single country still had not come into being at this point and was not to do so until 1871.

It was during this point we won our Indian Empire and lost our American one (which we shall come to later). Much of our success in India, despite competition with France, was due to the military skill of Robert Clive – who became Clive of India. Clive was a clerk with the East India Company who copied the French technique of training local inhabitants, whom they called Sepoys. They proved to be highly effective soldiers and they brought Clive a number of victories, notably at Arcot, and then at Plassey in 1757. Having defeated the French, Clive and a newly appointed Governor general, Warren Hastings, consolidated British power in India, ensuring that the whole country became a British possession.

France and Britain were also rivals in America. The first British colonies, the New England States, had been founded by puritans. Known as the Pilgrim Fathers, they had left England from Plymouth during James 1st's reign, in order to practise their religion without persecution. Actually, the early years of colonisation were much driven by religious conflicts. Catholics had taken refuge in Maryland, for example. These colonies were ruled by governors appointed by the English crown, but the British government did not itself interfere and left them pretty much to themselves. However, with French colonies in the south and in Canada, there was rivalry over control of the interior. The French began to build forts intended to contain the British. So, the then war minister, William Pitt, decided that an assault on the French was necessary and assigned James Wolfe to lead it. Despite what appeared to be an unassailable French position on the St Lawrence River, Wolfe led his men under cover of darkness into a position from where they could overwhelm the French, which they did. This was the Battle of Quebec of 1759. All Canada was taken from France, which formally ceded it in the Treaty of Paris of 1763.

While France held Canada, the British colonists were glad of British rule. Once that threat was removed, feelings changed. They fretted against the trade restrictions imposed on them – largely to protect trade in Britain. The final straw was when, in 1765, Britain imposed the Stamp Act, a tax to pay for the administration and military protection enjoyed by the colonies. The colonists responded by refusing to buy British goods and in 1773, when British tea arrived in ships, the ships were boarded and the tea tipped into the harbour. Those involved were dubbed the Boston Tea Party. Shortly after that, British troops were fired on. Thus began the American war of Independence which lasted seven years. In 1776, The American Declaration of Independence was signed. At that time, it was virtually impossible to fight a major war at that distance, a situation not helped by under-resourced generals. The London government was reluctant to commit much in the way of men and armaments to the colony and regarded the West Indies – whose commercial value at that time was far greater than that of America – as more important. Then France decided to avenge the defeats in Canada and blockaded the American coastal ports, meaning that fresh troops and supplies could not reach the British forces. After the Battle of Yorktown in 1781, in which the French navy and the colonist army defeated General Cornwallis, Britain formally granted independence to the colonies in 1782. In some respects, the American War of Independence could be regarded, at least in part, as a civil war. About a third of the colonists supported the British government and assisted British troops. However, after independence was finally granted, most of them went to Canada.

Colonial wars continued thereafter but the battles were far from Britain and often at sea. Indeed, during the latter part of the 18th century, British sea power grew with a change of battle tactics developed initially by Admiral Rodney and used by Admiral Nelson at Trafalgar (more of which, later). Another important naval development was the exploration of the southern Pacific Ocean by Captain James Cook who, in 1770, discovered Australia and New Zealand, and claimed them for the British Crown. The full value of these discoveries took some time to be realised but the discoveries were considered to be important, even at the time. Initially, Britain used the new lands as penal colonies, where what were considered to be undesirables were transported and dumped.

The French Revolution

It may seem odd to include reference to the French Revolution which took place between 1787 and 1799 but its repercussions affected this country greatly. Most significant was the rise of Napoleon Bonaparte, an artillery officer born in Corsica in 1769 and who rose to become Emperor. Actually, the revolution of 1799 was more of a coup d'état and through it Napoleon became Emperor. He then set about expanding his empire and soaked Europe in blood. He was a highly successful military leader and France was at war with Britain at the time anyway. In the main, this was the old story of colonial rivalry. The situation was made more volatile because France was allied with Holland, also a colonial rival. That said, Napoleon's main drive for conquests was focussed on adjacent countries in Europe. Indeed, by 1797, all the effective mainland opposition to Napoleon had been defeated and Britain alone remained.

Britain was saved by four able warrior leaders: three naval, one army. The first was Admiral Jervis, who in 1797 at St Vincent, destroyed a joint fleet of French and Spanish vessels while Admiral Duncan kept the Dutch fleet blockaded in port. Duncan deceived the Dutch, leading them to believe that a large fleet was waiting for them just offshore when, in fact, a large part of the British fleet had mutinied and the ships laid idle. His false signals kept the Dutch bottled up until the mutiny was resolved so that, when the Dutch did put to sea they were readily defeated.

Jervis' second in command was the son of a Norfolk clergyman: Horatio Nelson. When Napoleon went to Egypt with an invading expedition, his ships anchored in Aboukir Bay where, because of sandbanks nearby, they should have been safe. Nelson demonstrated magnificent tactical seamanship and attacked the French at night. One French ship blew up and all bar four French ships were captured or sunk. Thus, France's power in the Mediterranean was broken.

War was suspended in 1802 but broke out again in 1803. This time, Napoleon planned to invade Britain. This invasion had been anticipated and defences on the south coast had been built on the Kent and Sussex coast. A line of fortified Martello towers (54) had been built, together with a canal, known as the Royal Military Canal, cut parallel to the Kent coast from Hythe to Rye, which an invading army would have to cross. Furthermore, the French fleet was blockaded by British war ships anchored just outside the main ports of the French coast. Napoleon, ever the master tactician ordered one of his admirals, Villeneuve, to put to sail for the West Indies in the face of a storm, with the object of drawing off the British fleet. The ruse worked, but on his return he found himself attacked by Admiral Calder and afterwards found it necessary to put into Cadiz. Shortly afterwards, on 20th October 1805, the Franco-Spanish fleet moved out to the bay just off Cape Trafalgar where Admiral Nelson attacked them and, with the tactical brilliance he showed at Aboukir, again decisively defeated the French at the Battle of Trafalgar. Nelson himself was killed by a sniper during the battle. It was this battle which established British naval supremacy for many years afterwards. It also put an end to the threat of invasion by France. Nelson's ship, HMS Victory, lies in Portsmouth Naval Dockyard with an adjacent museum and is open to the public (55).

On land, Britain and France clashed on the Iberian Peninsula – Spain and Portugal. The British forces were led by General Sir Arthur Wellesley, the army commander in Portugal – later to become the Duke of Wellington. Wellesley pushed back the French forces until they were out of Spain altogether, losing not only territory but much manpower in the process. Seeking replacement conquests, in 1812, Napoleon then invaded Russia and advanced to the very

85

outskirts of Moscow. The Russians did not, however, sue for peace but let their two most valued defenders, "General January and General February" – the ferocious Russian winter – do the job for them. Harassed by Cossack cavalrymen as they retreated, the French army was cut to pieces and few survived. Napoleon's defeat cost him the French throne and, since European powers were keen not to make a martyr of him, he was sent into exile on the Isle of Elba (56).

Napoleon escaped from Elba, returned to France and raised another army. This time, he decided to invade Belgium. Britain and Prussia decided that there would be no peace while Napoleon could carry on his invasions. No-one was safe. Wellesley – by then Lord Wellington – was sent to Belgium to join with the Prussian army and settle the matter once and for all. Wellington's plan was to meet the oncoming French army just south of Brussels at Waterloo (57), a small town which is easy to find. Good military planning and the confidence Wellington and Blucher, the Prussian commander, had in each other, brought on 18th June 1815, the decisive victory that was needed to defeat Napoleon finally. On his return to Britain, a grateful country made him Duke of Wellington and Napoleon was exiled to St Helena (58) in the South Atlantic. There was to be no further escape: Napoleon died there on May 5th 1821.

Tourists can travel to Waterloo quite easily and guides around the battlefields – in English as well as French – are worthwhile. There is a Eurostar rail service from London to Brussels and there is easy onward transport for the few miles south to Waterloo village and battlefield.

The Industrial Revolution, Canals and Railways

In 1700, England and Scotland were agrarian countries where farms sold their produce within a few miles' radius. Few people had any need to move about: many rural dwellers spent their entire lives without ever travelling more than five or ten miles away from their homes. Perhaps the earliest move away from this was the enclosure of farms, as they moved away from mediaeval traditions of common pasture and row and furrow arable farming. Farms then gradually began to allow the nature of the land and the local climate to dictate what crops they grew and what animals they raised. Added to this, the period saw the introduction of the turnip, a root vegetable, which was easy to grow and eminently suitable to feed to livestock, particularly cattle. As a result, instead of the mass slaughter of livestock in the late autumn, it became possible and economic to feed cattle over the winter and slaughter them as and when needed. The result was a huge increase in productivity of farms, and it meant that they had surplus crops and animals to sell, although they needed to buy in other crops and meat from elsewhere. Consequently, farm produce began to be sold in local town markets rather than consumed in the immediate locality. This specialisation of agriculture resulted in a huge increase in food production and availability. With this widening of agricultural trade came the widening of other trades, hanging on the agricultural coat-tails, as it were.

At that time, animals had been driven to market with other commodities carried by pack-horses. This became inadequate and canals were built. Using inland barges on canals meant that much larger quantities could be carried as well as fragile items such as crockery. With such fragile items, breakages were reduced to such an extent that sales prices fell dramatically. Gradually, a whole network of canals emerged. Such industry as there was gravitated towards places where access to the canal network was convenient and because of this reliable and much cheaper form of transport, commodities and manufactured goods became much cheaper. Many of these canals still exist, albeit that they are now used largely for leisure purposes. As a result of this invigoration of trade, the economy grew.

In the mid-late 18th century, important discoveries were made. It was discovered how to use coal in iron smelting instead of charcoal. Consequently, the iron trade moved away from places where there was a good supply of wood for making charcoal and relocated near sources of coal. In particular, the Severn Gorge (59), near Ironbridge, Shropshire, had both iron and coal locally as well as the river for transport and it quickly became an industrial centre. Indeed, it is regarded as the cradle of the industrial revolution. Naturally, the area became busier and the ferries became inadequate, so a bridge had to be built. Completed in 1781, the bridge was the first cast-iron bridge ever constructed. The bridge is still in use and many of the early buildings still present. The whole area has been made into a huge museum which welcomes visitors. Ironbridge is close to the town of Telford.

What came next was steam. Discovered by Thomas Newcommen in 1712, steam was used as a source of power from then on, but it was limited in application. Steam was fed into a cylinder under a piston at low pressure. It was then cooled with cold water, creating a partial vacuum. Atmospheric pressure then pushed the piston downwards. This was adequate for large, static power and served in mines, mills etc. Many pioneers experimented with steam engines: Matthew Boulton and Richard Trevithick in particular but, although improvements were made, it was not until James Watt discovered how to make a high-pressure steam engine that a real breakthrough was made. Watt's version of the steam engine used far less coal and far less water. Not only was the engine itself smaller, but the reduced consumption of coal and water made it practical to carry enough on a vehicle for a journey. Thus began the age of powered transport beginning with the birth of the railways as well as the mechanisation of agriculture.

The development of steam power created a need for manufacturers to provide a reliable measure of the capability of the engines on offer, particularly since buyers would use them to replace horses. How many horses could an engine replace? Measurements were taken of the capability of a horse and a standard measure established: a horse could raise 550lbs through one foot in one minute. This became the standard measure of mechanical power output until very recently: the horsepower.

For many centuries beforehand – some as early as 1500 AD – mines had used trackways, in which horse-drawn wheeled wagons ran along rails (originally of wood but later of iron), usually from the mine head to the canal side. The development of Watt's steam pressure engine meant that horses could be replaced by a steam locomotive. That is exactly what, in 1814, George Stephenson did for the Killingworth colliery. Then in 1825, he opened the Stockton to Darlington Railway (60). At that stage, even though the building of railways spread, freight was the sole traffic. However, by the 1840s, passengers began to use the system. The people began to travel, much to the alarm of the aristocracy, who foresaw that the railways "would encourage the working classes to move about".

By 1850, the railways had reached the then outskirts of London and the end of each line was described as a terminus. Those original railway stations still exist and a London map which shows them also shows, consequently, the boundaries of London as they were at the time (61).

Shortly after this, in 1853, Britain was involved in the Crimean War, to prevent Russia from taking Turkey. The two battles of note are the attack by the British on Sevastopol and the Russian attack on Balaclava, which saw a number of cavalry charges by the British army, especially the notorious charge of the Light Brigade.

It is also remembered for the work of Florence Nightingale, who tended the wounded and established a hospital at Scutari. She was born in Florence, Italy, in 1820. She found that more soldiers died from disease than from war wounds and set about improving conditions, including nutrition and hygiene. Indeed, it was she who made nursing professional, and on her return, established a school of nursing. She died in London in 1910.

The advent of steam and the railways had several effects. First, power could be used for many manufacturing processes so cottage industries moved into large factories and the rural population followed from the country to the new industrial towns and cities. The cost of cloth, manufactured goods and agricultural produce fell, and towns and cities spread as it became both possible and economic to live outside the town centre and to travel to work by railway. Finally, these advances together made Britain the workshop of the world and wealthy with it, as manufactured goods were made in Britain and exported to the empire. Finally, it shifted wealth and power from the south to the north – from the agrarian communities of the southern counties to the industrial powerhouse in the northern cities.

Much of this revolution was encouraged by one monarch: in 1837, Queen Victoria ascended to the throne. She remained queen until 1901, our second longest-reigning monarch, having been overtaken by our present Queen Elizabeth 2nd. Queen Victoria's reign saw a period of prolific reform and invention as well as advancing industrialisation. Standards of living rose and the country at large – most people – became affluent. Just before her reign began, we saw the emancipation of Catholics, which gave them equal rights and allowed them to become civil servants, followed by the abolition of slavery.

To this was added the development of clippers – fast sailing ships servicing the tea and opium trades between England and China (The Cutty Sark, docked at Greenwich, is one such). This process was advanced by the invention of the telephone in 1874 by Alexander Graham Bell, the first stages of the invention of television in 1881 by Alan Campbell–Swinton and the invention in 1890 of the compression ignition engine – the diesel engine as we now refer to it – by Herbert Ackroyd-Stewart. Ackroyd-Stewart's engine was patented two years ahead of that invented by Rudolf Diesel and, where Diesel's engine – patented 1892 – ran on coal dust blasted into the cylinder by compressed air, Ackroyd-Stewart's engine ran on heavy oil (at this time it was referred to as rock oil (petra-oleum, petroleum) to differentiate it from whale oil) and had timed fuel injection. In other words, it was a crude version of the diesel engine we know today.

It was during the reign of Victoria that motor vehicles began to make their presence felt, not always to universal benefit. Many vehicles were based on farm traction engines and were predominantly steam-driven. Later, the motor car also made its appearance. The government was therefore moved to pass the Locomotive Act of 1861, which required powered vehicles to have a crew of three, including one who would walk 60 yards ahead of the vehicle, waving a red flag. It also imposed a speed limit of 4mph. This remained in force until 1896, when the speed limit was raised to 14mph and the red flag requirement was abolished. Motor vehicles continued to make an increasing impact on people's lives from then on. These early vehicles were steam powered but in August 1888, in Germany, Frau Bertha Benz established the spirit-fuelled motor car as a viable means of travel by her now famous journey from the family farm at Mannheim to Pforzheim.

Despite a very long period during which Queen Victoria was unseen in public while mourning following the death of Prince Albert, her husband, she was a popular queen for much of her reign. Her death, in 1901, was a shock to the nation. Most of those alive, indeed, everyone under the age of 64 –and it should be borne in mind that some two-thirds of the population at that time was under the age of thirty – had never known any monarch other than Victoria and there were fears for the monarchy. However, the monarchy's talent for continuity made its presence felt and Edward 7th was crowned. Much continued as before, which the nation found reassuring. Edward did not reign for long and in 1910, he died.

1910 was an important year for another development whose impact still reverberates today: The Balfour Declaration, when the British foreign secretary announced "His Majesty's government view with favour the establishment of a Jewish Homeland and will use their best endeavours to facilitate achievement of this object but, nothing shall be done to prejudice the civil and religious rights of non-Jewish communities or the rights and political status of Jews in other countries".

Then in 1911, a National Health Insurance Scheme was launched, the forerunner to the National Health system we know today, the latter having been introduced in 1948. Under the Scheme, employees pay into the NHS from their salaries and receive free medical care.

The Great War

On the death of King Edward, George 5th ascended to the throne. He is probably best known for having had to lead the country through the Great War, or World War One. The facts are well known but the actual blame cannot be attributed with certainty. The Habsburg heir to the Austrian throne, Franz Ferdinand, went to Bosnia to inspect and observe military manoeuvres. The day afterwards, 28th August 1914, he went to Sarajevo where, after one attempt at assassinating the Archduke (with a bomb) failed, a second attempt on his life was made by a Serbian nationalist, Gavrilo Princip, who shot both Archduke Ferdinand and his wife. Both died. In demanding "Justice", Austria's demands were excessive and opportunistic and the Serbian government hesitated. Thereafter, a series of interlocking alliances brought most of Europe into conflict.

From here on follows a summary of WW1, the Great War. For the student requiring more detailed history, there are many excellent books written by distinguished military historians, some of whom are listed at the back of this book.

A dangerous situation was made worse because Kaiser Wilhelm, Emperor of the newly-formed state of Germany, saw an opportunity to exact further punishment on France, a territorial and economic rival. His mental state is sometimes called into question on the basis that he was recorded as having had "a difficult birth" – this being interpreted by some as suggesting a likelihood of brain damage. The Kaiser was, certainly, somewhat eccentric and occasionally childlike. The state of Germany as we know it had been formed only in 1871, the year after the Franco-Prussian war, so the whole episode might be charitably put down to the birth-pangs of a new state, finding its place in the world. The German military establishment had for some time had a plan for the future invasion of France. Drawn up by General Schleiffen in 1910, it envisaged advance through Belgium and formation of a line along the Franco-Belgian border. That line would then advance into France and the western flank would sweep round quickly to the south and then east as the western flank advanced southwards then westwards and to form an encircling noose round Paris. The schedule envisaged the invasion taking six weeks.

Britain had a loose alliance (the "Entente Cordiale" of 1904) with France, which concerned itself primarily with containing the scope for conflict over colonial matters but it was seen to oblige Britain to give assistance to France if she were invaded. A British expeditionary force was sent and met the German forces near the River Marne. The Battle of the Marne effectively scuppered the Schleiffen plan by stopping the advance of the German west flank. Thereafter, each side tried to turn the flanks of the other and, to prevent that, each side extended its lines westward to the Belgian coast. This part is sometimes referred to as the race to the sea. The French army did likewise with the German southern flank and, eventually, the opposing lines extended from the Swiss border northwards to Verdun in eastern France, then swung north westerly towards Niewport – halfway along the coast between Dunkerque and Ostende.

In effect, this punctured the image of invincibility of the German army and forced its commanders to rethink the original plans. Thereafter, stalemate ensued for over four years. WW1 is often portrayed as a bloody waste led by incompetent and callous generals aided by aristocratic officers. The fact that the head of the British Armed Forces, Chief of Imperial General Staff, General Sir William Robertson had started his military career as a private soldier is often forgotten. It should also be remembered that senior officers have specific jobs to do, in planning and implementing operations, procuring supplies and ammunition and generally managing the army they command, so that some distance behind the front line is the proper place for them. Nevertheless, far from being safely away from the action, some 34 British generals were killed in those four years – more than in WW2 – and the most dangerous rank to hold was that of captain. It was not seen as a waste at the time: public perception remained positive until well after the death of the Field Marshall Haig in 1928. Then, several politicians, Lloyd George in particular, published self-exculpatory accounts of their respective roles. To begin with, much was new, in that war had not before been waged on such a scale and each side had a learning process to endure. WW1 might be described as the last war of the 19th Century or the first of the 20th., or both. Indeed, tactics and equipment changed steadily throughout the war, as developments and counter-developments arose. It is worthy of note that whilst the "butcher's bill" was huge, numerically, by virtue of the vast number of troops involved, many subsequent battles, including the WW2 Normandy landings, sustained proportionately greater losses.

Both sides drew similar conclusions, that a breakthrough of the opposing lines was necessary and that the most likely area where that might happen would be where the opposing lines curved in north-eastern France near the Belgian border, loosely between Ypres in Belgium and Lille in France. Over the ensuing years the great battles of WW1 were fought here: The Somme, Ypres, Passchendaele, Verdun.

The war progressed with, in general, the British and French forces gaining ground slowly but at considerable cost. The British army was led, first, by Sir John French and later Sir Douglas Haig. One problem both generals faced was that the British army was not, at that time, up to much. The army was secondary – little more than a colonial gendarmerie – since the two prime military objectives for most of the 19th century and into the early 20th were to keep our trade routes and sea lanes open and to guard against invasion. Anyone contemplating invading Britain or closing a sea lane had to confront the Royal

Navy, at that time the most powerful navy in the world. Consequently, Haig, in particular, had to grapple with the problem of training a citizen army to the level of skilled warriors while at the same time fighting a war against a formidable enemy. At the same time, weaponry and warfare itself changed rapidly. Germany's army, conversely, was a regular army of considerable size and good training. An additional difficulty is that Haig had to fight a coalition war: the military position of the French army sector, as well as political developments in both countries, had to be taken into account. For example, in 1916, the Battle of the Somme was as much an effort to draw enemy resources away from Verdun – where the French army fought a desperate battle to defend the town – as it was to take territory from the enemy. Likewise, assaults had to be launched to keep pressure off the French army during the mutinies of 1917. The French army saw several commanders over the duration of the war: Joffre, Nivelles, Petain and finally, Foch.

1917 was also the year of the October Revolution. The Revolution – and by extension – communism – was foisted on Russia by the German General Erich von Falkenhayn. He provided passage from Switzerland to St Petersburg to Lenin, Trotsky and their cohorts, with the express intention of fomenting revolution and causing Russia to collapse. That would lead, he knew, to a separate armistice with Russia and enable Germany to move large numbers of troops from the eastern front to fight against the British and the French – and the coming Americans.

America was brought into the war by German miscalculation. The strategy had been to prevent supplies getting to Britain from the USA and at first this was at least partly successful. However, when America was suspected of sending supplies under its own flag, the German U-boats sank a number of US merchant ships. America had no option. Like the British army in 1915, the American army, quite small, was not much of a fighting force. It had to be brought up to scratch and, when the first units arrived in June 1917, they were of no military significance. Indeed, even into early 1918, the insistence of General Pershing that none of his troops be deployed until he deemed them ready – and that they fight on their own sectors independently of the French and British armies, caused Allied commanders to wonder if the Americans were more of a hindrance than a help. Consequently, the relationship between General Pershing and the other Army commanders was tense. Certainly, during the German spring offensive in April 1918, the British army had to rely largely on its own resources. Fortunately, the German army had shot its bolt, was held and then pushed back steadily until in the autumn, the German high command – the Kaiser, von Hindenburg, von Falkenhayn and Ludendorff – had to recognise that they could do no more. The armistice of November 11th, 1918 then followed, despite the opposition of General Pershing. General Pershing's view – and subsequent events proved him right – was that it would be better to continue the war until the enemy was pushed back onto home soil, so that the German population would see their army defeated. Unfortunately, because of Pershing's past behaviour, his fellow commanders were suspicious of his motives and his idea was not accepted. Pershing's judgement was, nevertheless, proven sound inasmuch as a defeat in Germany on home soil rather than on foreign, would have forestalled the fiction promulgated by later German politicians – notably by Adolf Hitler – that Germany's army was not defeated but stabbed in the back by Marxists and Jews. Actually, Adolf Hitler was not even German: he remained an Austrian citizen until 1938.

As a consequence of the Great War, three of the four empires involved, collapsed: the Habsburg empire of Austria-Hungary, the Russian empire and the German empire. Only the British empire survived. By the end of the war, losses were horrendous: Britain and the Empire had lost 900,000 men and France 1,500,000. Germany had lost 3,500,000 and Russia had lost 17,000,000. Total losses were almost 23 million, added to which there were, probably, about three times that number wounded, probably never to work again. Such numbers were unprecedented but there was worse to come. An epidemic of influenza struck – or, more correctly called a pandemic. It was called Spanish Flu at the time, for even then the ability of the flu virus to mutate into new strains was known. It is now known as H1N1 and it had some peculiarities. To begin with, it was at its most virulent during the summer and autumn and it seemed to affect healthy young adults rather than the weak and elderly. Returning soldiers, being close together for much of their time, were particularly hard hit because their very proximity allowed the virus to spread. The pandemic wiped out 50,000,000 worldwide. Whilst it is associated with the Great War, the pandemic killed about 250,000 in Britain and 400,000 in France. In general, about 10% of victims died – some very quickly and it wiped out 3-5% of the world population.

That left, in Britain, an imbalance between the marriageable-age sexes. Of the 9.25 million people of marriageable age before the war, split roughly 50:50 by gender, at the end, just over 4.6 million young women had to compete for, perhaps, 3.25 million marriageable young men. In that figure, further allowance has to be made for men who survived the war but whose injuries rendered them unable to work or to support a wife, and therefore by the norms and customs of the day, un-marriageable. This reversed competition gave rise to the fashions and dances which were characteristic of the 1920s: the "Roaring Twenties". Whilst there are some parallels with the 1960s and its flowering of youth and youth culture, the sixties involved not the generation who had survived the war but the children of that generation.

During the war, in 1916, extreme nationalists in Ireland rebelled and in an attack on public buildings in Dublin, took over several of them, notably the Post Office building. The uprising was put down – perhaps more brutally than it would have been in peacetime, but there were elements of treason involved: assistance had been sought – and secured – from Germany. In the main, the Irish population, who at that time wanted no more than the level of autonomy given to other white colonies, resented the rebels for bringing trouble down on everyone's head but it caused rumblings of more serious discontent in the six counties of the north – the ancient kingdom of Ulster, those whom the Romans had identified as the "Scotiae". Whereas the south of Ireland – now the Republic of Ireland – is predominantly catholic, the north is staunchly protestant and the Ulster Protestants made plain their strong desire to remain under the arrangement of the 1800 Act of Union; that is, as an integral part of Britain. Protestants in the six counties outnumber Catholics by about 2:1.

North Sea

HOLLAND

• Ostend

Dunkirk

Ypres

• Calais

• Passchendaele

BRUSSELS

BELGIUM

Loos •   • Lens

• Vimy
        • Cambrai
• Bapaume   • Le Cateau

FRANCE

• Compiègne   Verdun

Key:

— — —   Front Line Nov. 1918

- - - - -   Franco - Belgium Border

—————   Front Line 1914

Civil War was threatened. To forestall this, Ireland was partitioned in 1920 and then, in 1921, the south became the Irish Free State and self-governing. Full independence as a republic was achieved in 1948.

Until recently, the Irish Republican constitution included a claim to the six counties of the north and is suspected of having encouraged the extreme republican element among the catholic minority in Ulster to engage in a campaign of violence and bombing to achieve union with the south. This constitutional claim was abandoned when the opposing extremists among the protestant majority made clear that their campaign of violence would extend to the streets of Dublin. Apart from the occasional outrage by one side or the other, the six counties of the north are now at peace.

The British economy took many years to recover from the First World War, as factories which had been devoted to war production adjusted to peacetime, former soldiers came home and had to adapt to civilian life, and the government of the day grappled with the huge financial cost and accumulated debts of the war. Consequently, there were frequent disputes over pay and conditions, the process made worse, perhaps, because the trades unions were encouraged by the various socialist and Marxist revolutions that were taking place in mainland Europe. The situation was made more difficult by the Wall Street crash of 1929, which triggered a depression throughout the rest of the world.

In May 1926, an attempt to reduce the wages of the miners brought them out on strike. By the 4th May, the Trades Union Congress, the over-arching body of the trades unions, called for a general strike. The government reacted somewhat harshly, supported by many who feared a Communist revolution similar to that endured by Russia. Fear of communism was rife in the country, exacerbated by a faked letter published by the Daily Mail, which urged the masses to start an uprising. The letter became known as the Zinoviev letter, after its supposed author. The middle classes reacted by running trains and buses and by getting power stations into operation. There was some conflict with the strikers but, on 11th May, the Trades Union Congress called off the strike.

By 1932, the UK's world trade had fallen by half and there were 2.5 million unemployed, out of an overwhelmingly male workforce much smaller than it is today. Britain was not in a strong position to resist the ravages of the depression, not having recovered economically from WW1. Naturally, the Left thought that its time might have come and agitated for a communist revolution. They did make gains but far less than might have been expected. In the end, the British government had to abandon the Gold Standard – under which the value of the £sterling was tied to the value of gold and that abandonment allowed recovery to take hold from 1933, albeit a slow one.

The Suffragettes

The campaign for women's rights began in 1866 with a petition to Parliament by Barbara Bodichaud. The baton was taken up by Emmeline Pankhurst in 1903 and after the Bill for women's rights was filibustered – talked out of the debate by Members of Parliament who gave such long speeches that the House ran out of time – the movement became much more militant. Women chained themselves to railings, went on hunger strikes when imprisoned and even died when, at Epsom racecourse, Emily Wilding Davison ran in front of the King's horse, which put considerable pressure on Parliament to improve matters. In the end, it worked and the Representation of the People Act was passed in 1918. A year later, Nancy Astor became the first woman to enter parliament as a Member of Parliament.

The Abdication

King George 5th died in 1936 and was succeeded by Edward 8th. Edward had been something of a playboy and, in political and social affairs, something of a loose cannon. Before the death of his father, he had been engaged in an affair with a married woman, an American called Wallis Simpson. He now wanted to marry her once she was divorced. That divorce would not be her first. That was quite simply not acceptable to the country – then socially much more conservative than it is today – to the people, to the church or to the Government, so Edward had to choose between this woman and his crown. He chose Mrs Simpson and abdicated on 11th December 1936. When they married, they became the Duke and Duchess of Windsor. Since it was likewise impossible for him to stay in Britain, the couple went to Paris and lived most of the rest of their lives there.

World War 2

Edward was succeeded by George 6th, a man who never expected – or wanted – to become King. He lacked personal confidence and had a terrible stammer but, with the support of his wife, Queen Elizabeth, overcame his difficulties and led his country exceptionally well until his death in 1952. King George 6th led his country and, with the help of Sir Winston Churchill, also an inspirational leader, kept up the morale of the country throughout the dark days of World War2. After the death of the King, Queen Elizabeth became the Queen Mother and was much loved by the nation until her death, at the age of 101, in 2001. The Queen Mother is remembered particularly fondly for a remark she made after Buckingham Palace – where the King and Queen stayed throughout the war – was hit by an enemy bomb, and she observed that she was pleased that the Palace had been hit, because it placed them on an equivalent footing with so many Londoners – she "could look the East End in the face" – a reference to the damage sustained in East London.

From 1933 onwards, British eyes had been cast nervously towards Germany and political developments there. Consequently, in 1936, moves were made to rearm and build up the army, navy and air force. Germany had fallen under the spell of an Austrian demagogue, Adolf Hitler, who was determined to lead Germany into war, the primary objective being to expand German territory and reinstate the First Reich, the Habsburg empire of 1375-1648. In 1939, Britain along with other countries, issued an ultimatum to Germany threatening war if Poland was invaded. Thus war began and British troops went to France and Belgium to contain the threat. They were driven off, but 350,000 soldiers were rescued off the coast at Dunkirk by small ships sent from England. An invasion of Britain was planned but what is called the Battle of Britain, between the Royal Air Force and the Luftwaffe saw, in mid-September 1940, the Royal Air Force victorious in that the Luftwaffe failed to establish air superiority over British skies, a critically important pre-condition for the invasion. That invasion – Operation Sea lion – was abandoned. After much success by German troops, the tide turned in 1943, the turning point being the Battle of Stalingrad in Russia. Bombing raids over Germany took their toll, including particularly daring raids on Berlin itself and on the dams which provided the hydro-electric power to the Ruhr valley – the industrial heartland of Germany. This latter was the famous "Dambusters" raid. Eventually in June 1944, Allied troops from Britain and the USA invaded and established bridgeheads on the Normandy coastline and proceeded to advance until, on May 7th 1945, Germany surrendered. Adolf Hitler and his wife – a few days after their marriage in the Reichstag bunker – had committed suicide on April 30th. The war in the Far East continued until August 1945 but was brought to an end by the United States Air Force, who dropped two atomic bombs, one on Hiroshima and the other on Nagasaki.

The shape of Europe changed radically after the war, with much of Eastern Europe under Soviet dominion – "behind the Iron Curtain" – and with Russia and the United States confronting each other with nuclear weapons. England suffered acute shortages after the war, which is now remembered as the period of rationing, when food, clothing and luxuries were in limited supply. Demand was controlled by the issue of ration books which had to be produced on each occasion when purchases were made.

We finally come to the post-war period, starting with the 1950s to the present time. Indeed, the lifetime of the author. However, exciting as they are, events of this late period are too recent to be evaluated with objectivity, and reporting on the history of our time is better left to historians of the future. However, it is worth mentioning the death of King George 6th in 1952 and the accession and coronation in 1953 of our present queen, Queen Elizabeth 2nd and her consort husband, Prince Philip, the Duke of Edinburgh, now both over 90 years of age. We now have four living generations of Royalty: Her majesty the Queen and Prince Philip; their oldest son and heir to the throne, Charles, Prince of Wales; his elder son Flight Lieutenant William Wales, Duke of Cambridge, the Duchess Catherine and their three children.

Text of the
Magna Carta of 1215

John, by the Grace of God, King of England, Lord of Ireland Duke of Normandy and Aquitaine, and Count of Anjou to the Archbishops, Bishops, Abbots, Earls, Justiciars, Foresters, Sheriffs, Stewards, servants, and to all his bailiffs and faithful subjects, greeting.

Know that, having regard to God and for the salvation of our soul, and those of our ancestors and heirs, and unto the honour of God and the advancement of the Holy Church and for the reform of our realm, by advice of our venerable fathers, Stephen, Archbishops of Canterbury, Primate of all England and Cardinal of the Holy Church, Henry, Archbishop of Dublin, William of London, Peter of Winchester, Jocelyn of Bath and Glastonbury, Hugh of Lincoln, Walter of Worcester, William of Coventry, Benedict of Rochester, bishops: of master Pandulf, sub-deacon and member of the household of our Lord the Pope, of brother Aymeric, master of the Knights of the Temple in England and the illustrious men William Marshall, Earl of Pembroke, William Earl of Salisbury, William Earl of Arundel, Alan of Galloway (Constable of Scotland), Waren Fitz Gerald, Peter Fitz Herbert, Hubert de Burgh, Seneschal of Poitou, Hugh de Neville, Matthew Fitz Herbert, Thomas Basset, Alan Basset, Philip d'Aubigny, Robert of Roppesley, John Marshall, John Fitz Hugh and of other faithful subjects.

1. In the first place we have conceded to God, and by this our present charter confirmed for us and our heirs for ever that the English church shall be free and shall have her rights entire and her liberties inviolate; and we wish that it be thus observed. This is apparent

from the fact that we, of our pure and unconstrained will, did grant the freedom of elections, which is reckoned most important and essential to the English Church, and did by our charter confirm and did obtain the ratification of the same from our lord, Pope Innocent III, before the quarrel arose between us and our barons. This freedom we will observe, and our will is that it be observed in good faith by our heirs for ever.

We have also granted to all freemen of our kingdom, for us and our heirs for ever, all the liberties written hereunder, to be had and held by them their heirs for ever

2. If any of our earls or barons, or others holding of us in chief by military service shall have died, and at the time of his death shall be of full age and owe relief, he shall have his inheritance on payment of the ancient relief, namely the heir or heirs of an earl, one hundred pounds for a whole earl's barony; the heir or heirs of a baron, one hundred pounds for a whole barony; the heir or heirs of a knight, one hundred shillings at most for a knight's fee; and whoever owes less, let him give less, according to the ancient custom of fiefs.

3. If, the heir of any of the aforesaid has been under age and in wardship, let him have his inheritance without relief and without fine when he comes of age.

4. The guardian of the land of an heir who is under age, shall take from the land of the heir nothing but reasonable produce, reasonable customs and reasonable services, and that without destruction or waste of men or goods; and if we have committed the wardship of the lands of any such minor to the sheriff, or to any other who is responsible to us for its issues, and he has made destruction or waste of what he holds in wardship, we will take of him amends and the land shall be committed to two lawful and discreet men of that fief who shall be responsible for the issues to us or to him whom we shall assign them; and if we have given or sold the wardship of any such land to anyone and he has thereupon made destruction or waste, he shall lose that wardship, and it shall be transferred to two lawful and discreet men of that fief, who shall be responsible to us in like manner, as aforesaid.

5. The guardian, so long as he has the wardship of the land, shall maintain the houses,

fishponds, weirs, mills, and other things pertaining to the land, out of the revenues of that land; and he shall restore to the heir when he has come to full age, all his land, stocked with ploughs and waynage, according as the season of husbandry requires, and with the revenues from the land can reasonably support.

6. Heirs shall be married without disparagement. However, before a marriage takes place, it shall be made known to the heir's next of kin.

7. A widow, after the death of her husband, shall forthwith and without difficulty have her marriage portion and inheritance. She shall not give anything for her dower, or for her marriage portion, or for the inheritance which her husband and she held on the day of the death of that husband. She may remain in the house of her husband for forty days after his death, within which time her dower shall be assigned to her.

8. No widow shall be compelled to marry, so long as she prefers to remain without a husband, always provided she give assurance that she will not marry without our consent, if she holds land from us, or else without the consent of whichever other lord from whom she holds her lands.

9. Neither we nor our bailiffs shall seize for any debt any land or rent so long as the chattels of the debtor are sufficient to pay the debt. Nor shall those that pledged sureties for the debtor be distrained so long as the principal debtor himself is able to satisfy the debt. If the principal debtor fails to pay the debt, having nothing wherewith to pay it, then the sureties shall answer for it. They shall have the lands and rents of the debtor, if they desire them until they are reimbursed for the debt they have paid for him, unless the principal debtor can show proof that he has discharged his obligations to them.

10. If one who has borrowed from Jews any sum great or small, dies before that loan shall be repaid, his heir shall pay no interest for so long as he remains under age, irrespective of from whom he holds his lands. If such a debt falls into our hands, we will take nothing but the principal sum in the bond.

11. And if anyone dies indebted to Jews, his wife shall have her dower and pay nothing

of that debt; and if any children of the deceased are left underage, necessaries shall be provided for them in keeping with the holding of the deceased. The debt shall be repaid out of the residue, save the service due to feudal lord. Let debts due to other than Jews be dealt with in a similar manner.

12. No scutage nor aid shall be imposed on our kingdom, unless by common counsel of our kingdom, except for the ransoming of our person, for making our eldest son a knight, and marrying our eldest daughter one time. For these, only a reasonable aid shall be levied. In like manner, it shall be done concerning aids from the city of London.

13. And the city of London shall have all its ancient liberties and free customs, by land as well as water. Furthermore, we decree and grant that all other cities, boroughs, towns and ports shall have their liberties and free customs.

14. And for obtaining the common consent of the kingdom concerning the assessment of an aid (other than as aforesaid) or of a scutage, we will cause to be summoned the archbishops, bishops, abbots, earls and greater barons, individually through letters. Moreover, all others who are our direct tenants, we will cause a general summons to be made by our sheriffs and bailiffs, for a fixed date after the expiry of forty days and at a fixed place. In all such letters of summons we will specify the reason for the summons. And when the summons has thus been made, business shall proceed on the day appointed, according to the counsel of such as are present, although not all who were summoned are present.

15. In future we will not grant any one licence to take an aid from his own free men, unless to ransom his person, to make his eldest son a knight and once to marry his eldest daughter. And on these occasions, only a reasonable aid shall be levied.

16. No man shall be compelled to do more service for a knight's fee or for any other land free-holding, than is due from it.

17. Common pleas shall not follow our court but shall be held in some fixed place.

18. Inquests of novel deseisin, morte d'ancestre and darrein presentiment shall only be held in their own county courts, in the following manner. We, or should we be out of the kingdom, our chief justice will send two justices to each county four times a year who, along with four knights of each county chosen by that county, shall hold the assize in the county, and on the day and in the meeting place of the county court.

19. If any of the said assizes cannot be held on the day of the county court, let there remain as many knights and freeholders, who were present at the county court on that day, as are necessary for the proper making of judgements, according to whether the business is more or less.

20. A freeman shall not be amerced for a trivial offence but only in accordance with the seriousness of his delinquency. And for a serious offence he shall be amerced in accordance with his delinquency, save his contenement. A merchant shall be amerced likewise, saving his merchandise and a villain shall be amerced likewise, saving his wainage – if they have fallen into our mercy. Such amercements shall not be imposed but by the oath of lawful and reputable men.

21. Earls and barons shall not be amerced but by their peers, and only in proportion to the degree of offence.

22. A clerk in holy orders shall not be amerced in respect of his lay holding except as aforesaid; further, his ecclesiastical benefice shall not be taken into account.

23. No vill or person shall be compelled to make bridges at riverbanks, except those who anciently were bound to do so.

24. No sheriff, constable, coroner, or other royal bailiff shall hold lawsuits meant to be held by royal justices.

25. All counties, hundreds, wapentakes and trithings shall remain at old rents, and without any increase, except at our demesne manors.

26. If anyone holding a lay fief from the Crown dies, and our sheriff or bailiff produces royal letters patent of summons for a debt owed to the Crown, it shall be lawful for our sheriff or bailiff to seize and catalogue chattels found in the lay fief of the deceased, to the value of the debt, as assessed by law-worthy men. Nothing at all shall be removed from there until the debt is fully paid. The residue shall be left to the executors of the will of the deceased. If there is no debt to the Crown, all the chattels shall go to the estate of the deceased, except reasonable shares for his wife and children.

27. If any freeman dies intestate, his chattels shall be distributed by his nearest kinsfolk and his friends, under supervision of the church, except that the rights of his debtors shall be maintained.

28. No constable or royal bailiff shall take corn or other provisions from any man without immediate monetary payment, unless the seller permits postponement.

29. No constable shall compel any knight to give money instead of castle-guard, if the knight is willing to do the guard himself, or supply another responsible man to do it, if he cannot do it himself for any reasonable cause. Further, a knight taken or sent on military service shall be excused castle-guard in proportion to the time he was in service.

30. No sheriff or royal bailiff, or any other person, shall take the horses or carts of any freeman for transport duty, except with the agreement of the said freeman.

31. Neither we nor our bailiffs shall take, for our castle, or for any other of our works, wood which is not ours, except with the agreement of the aforesaid freeman.

32. We will not hold the lands of those who have been convicted of felony beyond one year and one day. Then, the lands shall be returned to the lords of those fiefs.

33. Henceforth, all kiddles shall be removed from the Thames, the Medway and throughout all England, except at the sea coast.

34. The writ called praecipe, from henceforth, shall not be issued to any one regarding any

tenement whereby a freeman might lose the right of trial in his own lord's court.

35. There shall be one measure of wine, of ale and of corn, namely the London Quarter throughout our whole realm. There shall also be one width of cloth, be it dyed, russet or halberget; that is, two ells within the selvedges. Let weights be likewise singular throughout our whole realm.

36. Nothing shall be paid or taken henceforth for a writ of inquisition of life or limbs. Instead, it shall be given free of charge and not denied.

37. If a man holds Crown land by fee-farm, by socage or by burgage and also holds land of another lord for knight's service, we will not have the ward-ship of his heir or of such land as he holds of the other lord's fief. Nor shall we have ward-ship of that fee-farm, socage or burgage unless the fee-farm owes knight's service. We will not have ward-ship of a man's heir, nor of the land that the man holds through knight's service to someone else, because of any petty-sergeantry that he may hold from the Crown for the service of providing us daggers,, arrows or the like.

38. Henceforth, no bailiff shall place a man on trial upon his own word, without credible witnesses to support his word.

39. No freeman shall be arrested, or imprisoned or disseised or outlawed or exiled or in any other way harmed. No shall we proceed against him, or send others to do so, except according to Common Law.

40. To no one shall we sell, neither shall we refuse, or delay right or justice.

41. All merchants may leave or enter England in safety and security. They may stay and travel throughout England by road or water, free from all illegal tolls, in order to buy and sell according to ancient customs. This is except, in times of war, those merchants from the land which is at war with us. And if such merchants are found in our land at the beginning of the war, they shall be detailed, without injury to their bodies or goods until information is received by us or by our chief justiciar about in what way are treated

our merchants, thence found in the land at war with us. If our merchants are safe there, then so shall others be safe in our land.

42. It shall be lawful in future for anyone, keeping loyalty to the Crown, to leave our kingdom and to return safely and securely, by land and by water, except in time of war, when men may go only in the interest of our realm, for some short period and except those imprisoned or outlawed in accordance with the law of our realm, subjects of the country at war with us, and merchants, who shall be teared as aforesaid.

43. If anyone holding any escheat, such as the honour of Wallingford, Nottingham, Boulogne, Lancaster, or other escheats which are in our land and are baronies, dies, heir shall give only the relief and service to us that he would have given to the baron, if that barony had been in the baron's hands. We shall hold the escheat in the same manner in which the baron held it.

44. Men who dwell outside the forest henceforth need not come before our justiciars of the forest following a general summons, unless they are named in a plea or are sureties for any person or persons arrested for forest offences.

45. We will appoint us justices, constables, sheriffs, or bailiffs only those who know the law of the realm and who wish to observe it well.

46. All barons who have founded abbeys, for which they have charters from the kings of England, or for which they have long standing possession, shall have the custody of them when vacant, as they should have.

47. All forests that have been created in our reign shall be forthwith be dis-afforested, and similar course shall be followed for river-banks that we have made reserves during our reign.

48. All evil customs relating to forests and warrens, foresters, warreners, sheriffs and their officers, river-banks and their wardens, shall immediately be investigated in each county by twelve sworn knights of the same county, chosen by honest men of the county. The

evil customs shall, within forty days of the said inquest, be completely and irrevocably abolished. This is provided always that we are first informed, or our justiciar is informed if we should not be in England.

Text of the
Magna Carta 1225

Translated from the original Latin

Henry, by the Grace of God, King of England, Lord of Ireland, duke of Normandy and Aquitaine and Earl of Anjou to the archbishops, bishops, abbots, priors, earls, barons, sheriffs, governors, officers and all bailiffs, and his faithful subjects who see this present Charter, Greeting.

Know ye, that in the presence of God and for the salvation of our own soul and of the souls of our ancestors, and of our successors, to the exaltation of the Holy Church, and the amendment of our kingdom, that we spontaneously and of our own free will, do give and grant to the archbishops, bishops, abbots, priors, earls, barons, and all of our kingdom, these under-written liberties to be held in our realm of England for ever.

1. In the first place we grant unto God and by this our present Charter we have confirmed for us, and our heirs for ever, that the English church shall be free and shall have her whole rights and her liberties inviolable. We have also granted to all the free-men of our kingdom, for us and our heirs for ever, all the under-written liberties to be had and held for them and by their heirs, of us and our heirs.

2. If any of our earls or barons, or others who hold of us in chief by military service shall

die, and at his death his heir shall be of full age, and shall owe a relief, he shall have his inheritance by the ancient relief: that is to say, the heir or heirs of an earl, a whole earl's barony for one hundred pounds: the heir or heirs of a baron, a whole barony, for one hundred pounds: the heir or heirs of a knight, a whole knights fee for one hundred shillings at most: and he who owes less, shall give less, according to the ancient customs of fees. But if the heir of any such shall be under age, his lord shall not have the wardship of him nor of his land, before he shall have received his homage, and afterward such heir shall be in ward: and when he shall come to age, that is to say, to twenty and one years, he shall have his inheritance without relief and without fine: yet so, that if he be made a knight, whilst he is under age, his lands shall nevertheless remain in custody of his lord, until the term aforesaid.

3. The warden of the land of such an heir who shall be under age, shall not take from the lands of the heir any but reasonable issues, and reasonable customs and reasonable services, and that without destruction and waste of the men or goods. And if we commit the custody of any such lands to a sheriff, or to any other person who is bound to us for the issues of them, and he shall make destruction or waste upon the ward-lands, we will recover damages from him, and the lands shall be committed to two lawful and discreet men of the same fee, who shall answer for the issues to us or to him to whom we have assigned them: and if we shall give or sell to any one the custody of any such lands, and he shall make destruction or waste upon them, he shall lose that custody; and it shall be committed to two lawful and discreet men of the same fee, who shall answer to us in like manner as it is said before.

4. But the warden, as long as he hath custody of the lands, shall keep up and maintain the houses, parks, rabbit warrens, ponds, mills and other things belonging to the them, out of their issues: and shall restore to the heir, when he comes of full age, his whole estate, provided with carriages and all other things, at least such as he received it. All these things shall be observed in the custodies of vacant archbishoprics, bishoprics, abbeys, priories, churches and dignities, which appertain to us, excepting that these wardships are not to be sold.

5. Heirs shall be married without disparagement (a)

6. A widow, after the death of her husband, shall immediately and without difficulty have her freedom of marriage and her inheritance, nor shall she give any thing for her dower, or for her freedom of marriage, or for her inheritance, which her husband and she held at the day of his death: and she may remain in the principle messuage (b) of her husband, for forty days after her husband's death, within which time her dower shall be assigned: unless it shall have been assigned before, or excepting his house shall be a castle; and if she depart from the castle, there shall be provided for her a complete house in which she may decently dwell, until her dower shall be assigned to her as aforesaid and she shall have her reasonable estover (c) within a common term. And for her dower, shall be assigned to her the third part of all the lands of her husband, which were during his life, except she were endowed with less at the church door.

7. No widow shall be compelled to marry, whilst she is willing to live without a husband; but yet she shall give security that she will not marry, without our consent, if she hold of us, or without the consent of her lord if she hold of another'

8. Neither we nor our bailiffs, will seize any land or rent for any debt, while the chattels of the debtor present sufficient for the payment of the debt, and the debtor shall be ready to make satisfaction: nor shall the sureties of the debtor be distrained, whilst the principal debtor is able to pay the debt; and if the principal debtor fail in payment of the debt, not having wherewith to discharge it, or will not discharge it when he is able, then sureties shall answer for the debt; and if they be willing, they shall have the lands and rents of the debtor, until satisfaction be made to them for the debt which they had before paid for him, unless the principal debtor can show himself acquitted thereof against said sureties.

9. The City of London shall have all its ancient liberties, and its free customs as well by land as water. Furthermore, we will and grant to all other cities, and burghs and towns and the barons of the Cinque Ports, and all ports shall have all their liberties and free customs.

10. None shall be distrained to do more service for a knight's fee, nor for any other free tenement (d), than what is due from hence

11. Common pleas (e) shall not follow our court but shall be held in a fixed place.

12. Assizes upon writs of novel disseisin (f) and morte d'ancestre (g) shall not be taken but in their proper counties, and in this manner:- We, or our Chief Judiciary, if we should be out of the kingdom, will send judiciaries into every county, once in a year; who, with the knights of each county, shall hold in the county, the aforesaid assizes. And those things, which at the coming of the aforesaid judiciaries being sent to take the said assizes, cannot be determined, shall be ended by them in some other place in their circuit; and for those things which for difficulty of some articles cannot be determined by them, shall be determined by our judiciaries of the Bench, and there shall be ended.

13. Assizes of darrein presentment (h) shall always be taken before our judiciaries of the Bench, and there shall be determined.

14. A free man shall not be amerced (h) for a small offence but only to the degree of the offence; and for a great delinquency, according to the magnitude of the delinquency, saving his contenement: (i) and a merchant in the same manner, saving his merchandise and a villein (j), if he belong to another, shall be amerced in the same manner, saving to him his wainage (k), if he shall fall on our mercy: and none of the aforesaid amercements shall be assessed but by the oath of honest and lawful men of the neighbourhood. Earls and barons shall not be amerced but by their peers, and that only according to their delinquency. No ecclesiastical person (l) shall be amerced according to the quantity of his ecclesiastical benefice, but according to the quantity of his lay fee and the extent of his crime.

15. Neither a town nor any person shall be distrained to build bridges or embankments, except those which anciently, and of right, are bound to do it.

16. No embankments shall from henceforth be defended, but such as were in defence in the time of King Henry our grandfather; by the same places, and the same bounds as were accustomed to be in his time.

17. No sheriff, constable, coroners, nor other of our bailiffs, shall hold pleas of our crown.

18. If anyone holding of us a lay fee die, and the sheriff or our bailiff shall show our letter-patent of summons concerning the debt, which the deceased owed to us, it shall be lawful for the sheriff or our bailiff to attach and register all the goods and chattels of the deceased found on that lay fee, to the amount of that debt, by the view of lawful men. So that nothing is removed from thence until our debt is paid to us; and the rest shall be left to the executors to fulfil the will of the deceased; and if nothing be owing to us by him, all the chattels shall fall to the deceased, saving to his wife and children their reasonable shares.

19. No constable, nor his bailiff shall take the corn or goods of any one, who is not of that town where his castle is, without instantly paying money for them unless he can obtain a respite from the free will of the seller: but if he be of that town wherein the castle is, he shall give him the price within forty days.

20. No constable shall distrain any knight to give him money for castle guard, if he be willing to perform it in his own person, or by another reliable man, if he cannot perform it himself, for a reasonable cause: and if we do lead him or send him into the army, he shall be excused castle guard, according to the time that he shall be with us in the army, on account of the fee for which he hath done service in the host.

21. No sheriff or bailiff of ours nor any other person, shall take horses or carts of any, for the purpose of carriage, without paying according to the rate anciently appointed; that is to say, for a cart and two horses ten pence by the day, for a cart with three horse, fourteen pence by the day. No demesne (m) cart of any ecclesiastical person, or knight, or of any lord, shall be taken by the aforesaid bailiffs. Neither we, nor our bailiffs, nor those of any other, shall take another man's wood, for our castle, or for other uses, unless by the consent of him to whom the wood belongs.

22. We will not retain the lands of those who have been convicted of felony, excepting for one year and one day, and then they shall be given up to the lord of the fee concerned.

23. All kydells (n) for the future shall be quite removed out of the Thames and the Medway and through all England, excepting upon the sea coast.

24. The writ which is called "praecipe" (o) for the future shall not be granted to any one of any tenement by which a free man loses his court.

25. There shall be one measure of wine throughout all of our kingdom, and one measure of ale and one measure of corn, namely the quarter of London and one breadth of dyed cloth and of russets, and of halberjects (p), namely two ells within the selvedges.(q) Also it shall be the same with weights as with measures.

26. Nothing shall be given or taken(r) for a writ of inquisition, nor taken of him that request inquisition of life or limb; but it shall be given without charge, and not denied

27. If a man hold of us by fee-farm (s) or socage (t) or by burgage (u) and holds land of another by military service, we will not have the guardianship of his heir, nor of his land, which are of the fee of another, on account of that fee-farm, socage or burgage, unless the fee-farm owe military service. We will not have custody of the man's heir, nor the lands of anyone, which he hold of another by military service, on account of any petty-sergeantry (v) which he holds of us by the service of giving us daggers, or arrows, or the like

28. No bailiff, for the future shall put any man to his open law, nor to an oath, upon his own simple affirmation, without faithful witnesses produced for that purpose.

29. No free man shall be taken, or imprisoned, or dispossessed of his free tenement, or liberties, or free customs, or be outlawed, or exiled or in any way destroyed; nor will we condemn him, nor will we commit him to prison, excepting by the legal judgement of his peers, or by the law of the land. To none will we sell, to none will we deny, to none will we delay right or justice.

30. All merchants, unless they have before been publicly prohibited, shall have safety and security in going out of England, and in coming into England and in staying and in travelling through England as well by land as by water, to buy and sell, without any unjust exaction, according to ancient and right customs, excepting in time of war, and if they be of a country at war against us: and if such are found in our land at the

beginning of a war, they shall be apprehended, without injury of their bodies or goods, until it be known to us, or to our Chief Judiciary, how the merchants of our country are treated who are found in the country at war against us; and if ours be in safety there the others shall be in safety in our land.

31. If any man hold lands of any escheat (w), as of the honour (x) of Wallingford, Boulogne, Nottingham, Lancaster or of other escheats which are in our hand, and are baronies, and shall die, his heir shall not give any other relief, nor do any other service to us, than he should have done to the baron, if those lands had been in the hands of the baron; and we will hold it in the same manner that the baron held it. Neither will we have, by occasion of any barony or escheat, any escheat, or the custody of any of our men unless he who held the barony or escheat held otherwise of us in chief.

32. No free man shall, from henceforth, give or sell any more of his land, so that of the residue of his lands, the Lord of the fee may have the service due to him which belongeth to the fee.

33. All patrons of abbeys, which are held by Charters of Advowson (y) from the kings England, or by ancient tenure or possession of the same, shall have custody of them when they become vacant, as they ought to have, and such as it hath been declared above.

34. No man shall be apprehended or imprisoned on the appeal of a woman, for the death of any other man but her husband.

35. No County Court shall, from henceforth, be holden but from month to month; and where a greater term hath been used it shall be greater. Neither shall any sheriff or his bailiff, keep his turn in the hundred (z) but twice in the year; and no where but in due and accustomed place; that is to say, once after Easter, and again after the Feast of Saint Michael. And the view of frank-pledge (aa) shall be likewise at St Michael's term, without occasion; so that every man may have his liberties, which he had and was accustomed to have, in the time of King Henry our grandfather, or which he hath since procured him. Also the view of frank-pledge shall be so done, that our peace may be kept, and that the tything (bb) may be wholly kept, as it hath been accustomed; and

that the sheriff seek no occasions, and that he be content with so much as the sheriff was wont to have for his view-making, in the time of King Henry, our grandfather.

36. It shall not from henceforth be lawful for any to give his lands to any religious house, and to take the same land again to hold of the same house. Nor shall it be lawful to any religious house to take the land of any, and to lease the same to him from whom they were received. Therefore, if any from henceforth do give his land to any religious house, and thereupon be convict, his gift shall be utterly void and the land shall accrue to the lord of the fee

37. Scutage (cc) from henceforth shall be taken as it was accustomed to be taken in the time of King Henry, our grandfather. Saving to the archbishops, bishops, abbots, priors, Templars, Hospitallers, earls, barons, and all others, as well ecclesiastical as secular persons, the liberties and free customs which they have formerly had.

Also all those customs and customs and liberties aforesaid, which we have granted to be held in our kingdom, for so much of it as belongs to us, all our subjects, as well clergy as laity, shall observe towards their tenants as far as concerns them

And for this grant and gift of these liberties, and of the other contained in our Charter of Liberties of our Forest, the archbishops, bishops, abbots, priors, earls, barons, knights, free tenants, and all others of our kingdom, have given to us the fifteenth part of all their moveables. And we have granted to them for us and our heirs, that neither we nor our heirs shall procure or do any thing , whereby the liberties in this Charter contained shall be infringed or broken; and if any thing shall be procured by any person contrary to the premises, it shall he had of no force or effect.

Omitted: a listing of the names of witnesses to this charter

Given at Westminster, eleventh day of February, in the ninth year of our reign.

Glossary

a)   not to someone of a lower social status

b)   house and outbuildings

c)   the right to take wood for fuel, repairs etc

d)   land holding

e)   ordinary lawsuits

f)   recent interruption in the ownership of land

g)   an heir being deprived of his inheritance

h)   last person to appoint a clergyman to a vacant church

i)   livelihood

j)   feudal tenant

k)   implements, equipment, seed-corn and stock

l)   clergyman, priest, monk

m) land attached to a manor

n)   fish weirs

o)   right of trial in his own lord's court

p)   forms of rough cloth

q)   one ell: about 45 inches (1.143m)

r)   paid or accepted

s)   land held freehold but paying rent

t)   land held in exchange for periodic payments to the owner

u)   land rented from the owner

v)   minor service owed to the king

w) land reverting to a lord, on the death of the owner or holder, without heirs

x) large estate

y) the right to recommend or appoint a member of the clergy to a vacant benefice

z) a sub-division of a county

aa) the compulsory sharing of responsibility among persons bound by kinship or oath of fealty to a lord or knight

ab) the tything man or chief pledge, leader of the frank-pledge

ac) tenure of a knight's service: a tax payable to avoid military service

The Text of the
The Provisions of Oxford, 1258

The provision made at Oxford:

It has been provided that from each county there shall be elected four discreet and lawful knights who, on every day that the county (court) is held, shall assemble to hear all complaints touching any wrongs and injuries inflicted on any persons by sheriffs, bailiffs, or any other men, and to make the attachments that pertain to the said complaints until the arrival of the Chief Justiciar in those parts: so that they shall take from the plaintiff adequate pledges for his prosecution, and from the defendant for his coming and standing trial before the said Justiciar on his first arrival; and that the four knights aforesaid shall have all the said complaints enrolled, together with their attachments, in proper order and sequence – namely, for each hundred separately and by itself – so that the Justiciar, on his first arrival, can hear and settle the aforesaid complaints from each hundred. And they shall inform the sheriff that they are summoning all his hundred-men and bailiffs before the said Justiciar on his next arrival, for a day and a place which he will make known to them: so that every hundred-man shall cause all the plaintiffs and defendants of his bailiwick to come in succession, according to what the aforesaid Justiciar shall bring to trial from the aforesaid hundred; also as many men and such men – both knights and other free and lawful men – as may be required for best proving the truth of the matter, in such a way that all are not troubled at one at the same time; rather let as many come as can be tried and concluded in one day.

Also it is provided that no knight of the aforesaid counties, by virtue of an assurance that he is not to be placed on juries or assizes, shall be excused by a charter of the lord king or be exempt from this provision thus made for the common good of the whole kingdom.

Those chosen from the Lord King's side:

The lord bishop of London, the lord bishop elect of Winchester, the lord Henry, son of the king of Germany: the lord John, Earl de Warenne: the lord Guy de Lusignan; the Lord William de Valence; the lord John, earl of Warwick; the John Mansel; Brother John of Darlington the abbot of Westminster the lord Henry of Hengham

Those chosen from the side of the earls and barons

The lord bishop of Worcester, Walter de Cantilupe; the lord Simon, earl of Leicester; the lord Richard, earl of Gloucester; the lord Humphrey de Bohun, earl of Hereford; the lord roger marshal; the lord Roger de Mortimer; the lord John Fitz-Geoffrey; the lord Hugh Bigod; the lord Richard de Gray; the lord William Bardulf; the lord Peter de Montfort; the lord Hugh Despenser. And if it should happen that of necessity any one of these cannot be present, the rest of them shall elect whom they please in place of the absentee, namely, another person needful for carrying on that business.

Thus the community of England swore at Oxford

We make known to all people that we have sworn on the holy gospels and are held together by this oath, and promise in good faith, that each one of us together will help each other, both ourselves and those belonging to us against all people, doing right and taking nothing that we cannot take without doing wrong, saving faith to the king and crown. And we promise on the same oath that none of us will ever take anything of land or moveables whereby this oath can be disturbed or in any way impaired. And if any one so acts contrary to this, we will hold him as a mortal enemy.

This is the oath of the twenty-four

Each one swore on the holy gospels that he for the glory of God and in loyalty to the King and for the benefit of the kingdom will obtain and treat with the aforesaid sworn persons upon the reform and improvement of the condition of the kingdom. And that he will not fail for gift or promise, for love or hatred for fear of any one, for gain, for loss, loyalty to act according to the tenor of the letter that the king has given on this and his son likewise.

Thus swore the Chief Justiciar of England

He swears that he will well and loyally according to his power do what belongs to the justiciars office of dispensing justice to all men and for the profit of the king and kingdom, in accordance with the provision made and to be made by the twenty-four, and by the king's council and magistrate of the land, who will swear to help and support him in these things.

Thus swore the Chancellor of England

That he will not seal any writ except a writ of course without the order of the king and of the councillors who are present. Nor will he seal a gift of great ward-ship or of a large sum of money or of escheats without the assent of the full council or the greater part of it. And he will not seal anything that is contrary to what has been or will be ordained by the twenty-four or by the greater part of them. And that he will not take any reward otherwise that is agreed for others. And he will be given a companion in the way that the council will provide.

This is the oath taken by the wardens of the castles

That they will keep the king's castles loyally and in good faith for the use of the king and his heirs. And that they will give them up to the king or his heirs and to no other and through his council and in no other way; that is to say, through men of standing in the land elected to the council or through the greater part of them. And this part is to last full twelve years. And henceforth they shall not be prevented by this establishment and this oath from being able to give them up freely to the king and his heirs.

These are the men sworn of the king's council:

The archbishop of Canterbury; the bishop of Worcester; the earl of Leicester; the earl of Gloucester; the earl marshal; peter of Savoy; the count of Aumalke; the earl of Warwick; the earl of Hereford; John Mansel; John Fitz-Geoffrey; Peter de Montfort; Richard de Grey; Roger Mortimer; James Audley.

The twelve on the king's side have chosen from the twelve on the side of the community: the earl Roger Marshal and Hugh Bigod. And the party of the community has chosen from the twelve who are on the side of the king, the earl of Warwick and John Mansel

And these four have the power to elect the council of the king; and when they have made the election, they shall designate those to the twenty-four. And that shall hold on the majority of the four agree.

These are the twelve who have been elected by the barons, on behalf of the whole community of the land, to consider common needs along with the king's council at three annual parliaments;

The lord bishop of London, the earl of Winchester, the earl of Hereford, Philip Basset, John de Balliol, John de Verdun, John de Grey, Roger de Sumery, Roger de Mohaut, Hugh Dispenser, Thomas de Gresley, Giles d'Argentein.

These are the twenty-four appointed by the community to consider aid for the king;

The bishop of Worcester, the bishop of London, the bishop of Salisbury, the earl of Leicester, the earl of Gloucester, the earl marshal, Peter of Savoy, the earl of Hereford, the count of Aumale, the earl of Winchester, the earl of Oxford, John Fitz-Geoffrey, John de Grey, John de Balliol, Roger Mortimer, Roger de Sumery, Roger de Mohaut, Peter de Montfort, Thomas de Gresley, Fulk de Kerdiston, Giles d'Argentein, John Kyriel, Philip of Basset, Giles of Erdington.

And if any of these cannot or will not be present, those who are present shall have power to elect another in his place

Concerning the state of the Holy Church

It should be remembered that the state of the Holy Church is to be amended by the twenty-four chosen to reform the state of the kingdom of England – at what time and place they think best, according to the powers that they hold by writ of the king of England.

Concerning the Chief Justice

Furthermore that a chief justice – or two – shall be appointed; also what power he shall have; and that he shall be for only one year, so that at the end of the year he shall render account of his term before the king and the royal council and before the man who is to follow him.

Concerning the Treasurer and the Exchequer

The same with regard to the Treasurer; so that he shall render account at the end of the year. And according to the ordinance of the said twenty-four, other good men are to be appointed to the exchequer, whither all matters of the land are to come, and not elsewhere. And let that be amended which seems in need of amendment.

Concerning the Chancellor

The same with regard to the chancellor; so that he shall render account of his term at the end of the year, and that merely by the king's will, shall he seal nothing out of course but shall do so by the council that surrounds the king.

Concerning the power of the Justice and of the Bailiffs

The chief justice has the power to redress the misdeeds of all other justices, of bailiffs, of earls, of barons and of all other people, according to the rightful law of the land. And writs are to be pleaded according to the law of the land in the proper places. And the justices shall accept nothing unless it is a present of bread and wine and like things: namely, such meat and drink as have been customarily bought for the day for the tables of the chief men. And this same regulation shall be understood for all the king's councillors and all his bailiffs. and no bailiff, by virtue of his office or of some plea, shall take any fee, either by his own hand or in any manner through another person. And if he is convicted, let him be punished; likewise any man who gives. And the king, if suitable, shall give his fees to his justices and to his people who serve him so that they shall have no need of taking anything from others.

Concerning the sheriffs

As sheriffs there shall be appointed loyal persons, good men who are landholders; so that in each county there shall be as sheriff a feudal tenant of the same county, who shall well, loyally and justly treat the people of the county. And he shall take no fee: that he shall be sheriff for no more than a year and during that year he shall render his accounts at the exchequer and be responsible for his term; that the king, from royal income, shall make allowance to him in proportion to his receipts, so that he may rightly keep the county; and he shall take no fees, neither he nor his bailiffs. And if they are convicted, let them be punished.

It should be remembered that, with regard to the Jewry and the wardens of the Jewry, such reforms are to be established as shall carry out the oath in this respect.

Concerning the Escheators

Good escheators are to be appointed. And they shall take nothing from the goods of deceased persons whose lands ought to be in the king's hands; but that, if a debt is owing to him, the escheators shall have free administration of the goods until they have carried out the king's wishes – and this according to the provision in the charter of liberties. Also enquiry shall be made concerning the misdeeds committed there by escheators and that redress shall be made for such. Nor shall tallage (a tax) or anything else be taken, except as it should be according to the charter of liberties. The charter of liberties is to be strictly observed.

Concerning the exchange of London

It must be remembered to establish reforms touching the exchange of London, also touching the city of London and all other cities of the king, which have been brought to shame and ruin by tallages and other oppressions.

Concerning the household of the king and queen

It must be remembered to reform the household of the king and queen

Concerning the parliaments, as to how many shall be held annually and in what manner

It must be remembered that the twenty-four have ordained that there are to be three parliaments a year; the first on the octave of St. Michael, the second on the morrow of Candlemas and the third on the first day of June, that is to say, three weeks before Saint John (this means 6th October, 3rd February and

3rd June) to these three parliaments, the chosen councillors of the king shall come , even if they are not summoned, in order to examine the state of the kingdom and likewise the king; and by the king's command also at other times, whenever it is necessary. So to it should be remembered that the community is to elect twelve good men, who shall come to the three parliaments and at other times, when there is need and when the king and his council summon them to consider the affairs of the king and the kingdom. And the community shall hold as established whatever these twelve shall do – that is to reduce the cost to the community. Fifteen are to be named by these four men – that is to say by the earl marshal, the earl of Warwick, Hugh le Bigot and John Mansel – who have been elected by the twenty-four to name the aforesaid fifteen, who are to form the king's council. And they are to be confirmed by the aforesaid twenty-four, or by the greater number of those men. And they shall have the power of advising the king in good faith concerning the government of the kingdom and concerning all matter that pertain to the king or the kingdom; and of amending or redressing everything that they shall consider in need of amendment or redress. And they shall have authority over the chief justice and over all other people. And if they cannot be present, that shall be firm and established that which the greater number of them enact.

NB The original document has been lost and these provisions have been established from chronicles and other documents.

The English Bill of Right, 1689

An Act declaring the Rights and Liberties of the Subject and Settling the Succession of the Crown

Whereas the Lords Spiritual and Temporal and Commons assembled at Westminster, lawfully, fully and freely representing all the estates of the people of this realm, did on the thirteenth day of February in the year of our Lord one thousand six hundred and eighty-eight (a) present unto their Majesties, then called and known by the names William and Mary, Prince and Princess of Orange (b), being present in their proper persons, a certain declaration in writing made by the said Lord and commons in the words following:-

Whereas the late King James the Second, by the assistance of divers evil counsellors, judged and ministers employed by him, did endeavour to subvert and extirpate the Protestant religion and the laws and liberties of this kingdom;

By assuming and exercising a power of dispensing with and suspending laws and the execution of laws without the consent of Parliament;

By committing and prosecuting divers (c) worthy prelates for humbly petitioning to be excused from concurring to the said assumed power;

By issuing and causing to be executed a commission under a great seal for erecting a court called the Court of Commissioners for Ecclesiastical Causes;

By levying money for and to the use of the Crown by pretence of prerogative for other time and in other manner than the same was granted by Parliament;

By raising and keeping a standing army within his kingdom in time of peace without consent of parliament, and quartering soldiers contrary to law;

By causing several good subjects being protestants to be disarmed at the same time when papists were both armed and employed contrary to law;

By violating the freedom of election of members to serve in Parliament;

By prosecutions in the court of the King's Bench for matters and causes cognizable only in Parliament, and by divers other arbitrary and illegal courses;

And whereas of late years partial corrupt and unqualified persons have nee returned and served on juries in trials, and particularly divers jurors in trials for high treason which were not freeholders;

And excessive bail hath been required of persons committed in criminal cases to elude the benefit of the laws made for the liberty of the subjects;

And excessive fines have been imposed;

And illegal and cruel punishments inflicted;

Which are utterly and directly contrary to the known laws and statutes and freedom of this realm;

And whereas the said late King James the Second having abdicated the government and the throne being thereby vacant, His Highness the Prince of Orange (whom it has pleased almighty God to make the glorious instrument of delivering his kingdom from popery (d) and arbitrary power) did (by the advice of the Lords Spiritual and temporal and divers principal persons of the Commons) cause letters to be written to the Lords Spiritual and Temporal (e) being Protestants, and other letters to the several counties, cities, universities and cinque ports, for the choosing of such persons to represent them as were of right to be sent to Parliament, to meet and sit at Westminster upon the two and twentieth day of January in this year one thousand, six hundred and eighty-eight (a) in order to such an establishment as that their religion, laws and liberties might not again be in danger of being subverted, upon which letter elections have been accordingly made;

And thereupon the said Lords Spiritual and Temporal and Commons, pursuant to their respective letters and election, being now assembled in a full and free representative of this nation, taking into their most serious consideration the best means for attaining the ends aforesaid, do in the first place (as their ancestors in like case have usually done) for the vindicating and asserting their ancient rights and liberties declare:

That the pretended power of suspending the laws or the execution of the laws by regal authority without consent is illegal;

That the pretended power of dispensing with laws or the execution of laws by regal authority, as it hath been assumed and exercised of late, is illegal;

That the commission for erecting the late Court of Commissioners for Ecclesiastical Causes, and all other commissions and court of like nature, are illegal and pernicious;

That the levying of money for or to the use of the Crown by pretence of prerogative, without grant of Parliament, for longer time, or in other manner than the same is or shall be granted, is illegal;

That it is the right of the subjects to petition the king, and all commitments and prosecutions for such petitioning are illegal;

That the raising and keeping of a standing army within the kingdom in time of peace, unless it be with consent of Parliament, is against law;

That the subjects which are Protestants may have arms for their defence suitable to their conditions and as allowed by law;

That the election of members of Parliament ought to be free;

That the freedom of speech and debates or proceedings in Parliament ought not to be impeached or questioned in any court or place out of Parliament;

That excessive bail ought not to be required, nor excessive fine imposed, nor cruel and unusual punishments inflicted;

That jurors ought to be duly empanelled and returned, and jurors which pass upon menin trial for high treason ought to be freeholders;

That all grants and promises of fines and forfeitures of particular persons before conviction are illegal and void;

And for that for redress of all grievance, and for the amending, strengthening and preserving of the law, Parliament ought to be held frequently.

And they do claim, demand and insist upon all and singular the premises as their undoubted rights and liberties, and that no declarations, judgements, doings of proceedings to the prejudice of the people in any of the said premises ought in any wise to be drawn hereafter into consequence or example; to which demand of their rights they are particularly encouraged by the declaration of his Highness, the Prince of Orange as being the only means of obtaining the full redress and remedy therein.

Having therefore an entire confidence that his said Highness the Prince of Orange will perfect the deliverance so far advanced by him, and will still preserve them from violation of their rights which they have here asserted, and from all other attempts upon their religion, rights and liberties, the said Lords Spiritual and Temporal and Commons assembled at

Westminster do resolve that William and Mary, Prince and Princess of Orange, be declared King and Queen of England, France and Ireland and the dominions thereunto belonging, to hold the crown and royal dignity of the said kingdoms and dominions to them, the said Prince and Princess, during their lives and the life of the survivor to them, and that the sole and full exercise of regal power be only in and executed by the said Prince of Orange in the names of the said Prince and Princess during their joint lives, and their deceases the said crown and royal dignity of the same kingdoms and dominions to be to the heirs of the body of the said Princess, and for default of such issue to the Princess Anne of Denmark and the heirs of her body, and for default of such issue to the heirs of the body of the said Prince of Orange. And the Lords Spiritual and Temporal do pray the said Prince and Princess to accept the same accordingly.

And that the oaths hereafter mentioned be taken by all persons to whom the oaths have allegiance and supremacy might be required by law, instead of them; and that the said oaths of allegiance and supremacy be abrogated.

I, (name) do sincerely promise and swear that I will be faithful and bear true allegiance to their Majesties King William and Queen Mary. So help me God.

I (name) do swear from my heart abhor, detest and abjure as impious and heretical this damnable doctrine and position, that princes excommunicated or deprived by the Pope or any authority of the see of Rome may be deposed or murdered by their subjects or any other whatsoever. And I do declare that no foreign prince, person, prelate, state or potentate hath or ought to have any jurisdiction, power, superiority, pre-eminence or authority, ecclesiastical or spiritual, within this realm. So help me God.

Upon which their said Majesties did accept the crown and royal dignity of the kingdoms of England, France and Ireland, and the dominions thereunto belonging, according to the resolution and desire of the said Lords and Commons contained in this declaration. And thereupon their majesties were pleased that the Lords Spiritual and Temporal and Commons, being two Houses of Parliament should continue to sit, and with their Majesties royal concurrence make effectual provision for the settlement of the religion, laws and liberties of this kingdom, so that the same for the future might not be in danger again of being subverted, to which the said Lords Spiritual and Temporal and Commons did agree, and proceed to act accordingly.

Now in pursuance of the premises the said Lords Spiritual and Temporal and Commons in Parliament assembled, for the ratifying, confirming and establishing the said declaration and the articles, clauses matters and things therein contained by the force of law made in due form by authority of Parliament, do pray that it may be declared and enacted that all and singular the rights and liberties asserted and claimed in the said declaration are true, ancient and indubitable rights and liberties of the people of this kingdom, so shall be esteemed, allowed. Adjudged, deemed and taken to be; and that all and every the particulars of the aforesaid shall be firmly and strictly holden and observed as they are expressed in the said declaration, and all officers and ministers whatsoever shall serve their majesties and their successors according to the same in all time to come.

And the said Lords Spiritual and Temporal and Commons, seriously considering how it hath pleased Almighty God in his marvellous providence and merciful goodness to this nation to provide and preserve their said Majesties royal persons most happily to reign over us upon the throne of their ancestors, for which they render unto him from the bottom of their hearts their humblest thanks and praises, do truly, firmly, assuredly and in the sincerity of their hearts think, and do hereby recognize, acknowledge and declare that King James the Second, having abdicated the government and their Majesties having accepted the crown and royal dignity as aforesaid, their said majesties did become, were, are and of right ought to be by the laws of this realms our sovereign liege lord and lady, king and queen of England France and Ireland and the dominions thereunto belonging, in and to whose princely persons the royal state, crown and dignity of the said realms with all honours, styles, titles, regalities, prerogatives, powers, jurisdictions and authorities to the same belonging and appertaining are most fully rightfully and entirely invested and incorporated, united and annexed.

And for preventing all questions and divisions in this realm by reason of any pretended titles to the crown, and for preserving a certainty in the succession thereof, in and upon which the unity, peace, tranquillity and safety of this nation doth under God wholly consist and depend, the Said Lords Spiritual and Temporal and Commons do beseech their Majesties that it may be enacted, established and declared, that the crown and regal government of the said kingdoms and dominions, with all and singular the premises thereunto belonging and appertaining , shall be and continue to their said majesties and the survivor of them during their lives and the life of the survivor of them, and that entire, perfect and full exercise of the regal power and government be only in and executed by his Majesty in the names of both their majesties during their joint lives and after their deceases the said crown and premises shall be and remain to the heirs of the body of her Majesty and for default of such to her Royal Highness, the Princess Anne of Denmark and the heirs of the body of his said Majesty; and thereunto the said Lords Spiritual and Temporal and Commons do in the name of all the people aforesaid most humbly and faithfully submit themselves, their heirs and posterities for ever and do faithfully promise that they will stand to, maintain and defend their said Majesties, and also the limitation and succession of the crown herein specified and contained, to the utmost of their powers with their lives and estates against all persons whatsoever that shall attempt anything to the contrary.

And whereas it has been found by experience that it is inconsistent with the safety and welfare of this Protestant kingdom to be governed by a popish prince, or by any king or queen marrying a papist, the said Lords Spiritual and Temporal and Commons do further pray that it be enacted, that all and every person and person that is, are or shall be reconciled or shall hold communion with the see or church of Rome, or shall profess the popish religion , or shall marry a papist, shall be excluded and for ever incapable to inherit, possess, or enjoy the crown and government of this realm and Ireland and the dominions belonging to any part of the same, or to have, use or exercise any regal power, authority or jurisdiction within the same; and in all and every such case or cases the people of these realms shall and are hereby absolved of their allegiance; and the said crown and government shall from time to time descend to and be enjoyed by such person or persons being Protestants as should have inherited and enjoyed the same in case the said person or persons so reconciled, holding communion or professing or marrying as aforesaid were naturally dead; and that every king and queen of this realm who at any time hereafter shall come to and succeed in the imperial crown of this kingdom shall of the first day of the first Parliament next after his or her coming to the crown, sitting in his or her throne in the House of Peers (f) in the presence of the Lords and Commons therein assembled, on or at his or her coronation before such a person or persons who shall administer the coronation oath to him or her at the time of his or her taking the said oath (which shall first happen) make, subscribe and audibly repeat the declaration mentioned in the statute made in the reign of King Charles the Second, entitled "An Act for the more effectual preserving the king's person and government by disabling papists from sitting in either House of Parliament"

But if it shall happen that such a king or queen upon his succession to the crown of this realm shall be under the age of twelve years, then every king or queen shall make, subscribe and audibly repeat the same declaration at his or her coronation or the first day pf the meeting of the first Parliament as aforesaid which shall first happen after such a king or queen shall have attained the said age of twelve years. All of which their majesties are contented and pleased shall be declared, enacted and established by authority of this present Parliament, and shall stand, remain and be the law of this realm for ever; and the same are by their said Majesties, by and with the advice and consent of the Lords Spiritual and Temporal and Commons in Parliament assembled and by the authority of the same, declared, enacted and established accordingly.

II. And it be further declared and enacted by the authority of the aforesaid, that from and after this present session of Parliament no dispensation by "non obstante" (g)of or to any statute or part thereof shall be allowed of in such statute, and except in such cases as shall be specially provided for by and by one or more bill or bills to be passed during this present session of Parliament.

III Provided that no charter or grant or pardon granted before the three and twentieth day of October in the year of our Lord one thousand six hundred and eighty-nine shall be any ways impeached or invalidated by this Act, but that the same shall be and remain of the same force and effect in law and no other that if this Act has never been made.

(a) England still used the Julian Calendar until 1752: The first day of 1689 would have been 1st March. On this basis, the thirteenth February was still 1688.
(b) Prince of Orange, despite referring to the then Principality of Orange, in southern France, is the title of the heir to the Dutch throne.
(c) Various
(d) Catholicism
(e) Secular Lords, Archbishops and Bishops and members of the House of Commons

(f) House of Lords
(g) non obstante: "notwithstanding" allowing the king to override any law to the contrary.

Historical Locations: Where to See British History

If this is the reader's first trip to Britain, then it is perfectly possible to enjoy our history for the entire holiday without leaving London but, for those with more time, the provinces offer much that is fascinating and intriguing. Britain has a long history of being populated and it is virtually impossible to go anywhere without finding something of historical interest. The problems become not where to go – but where to stop. Travel by train is quite efficient and comfortable provided the peak hours are avoided. Travel by road is less easy but often easier than the alternative: our density of population sometimes bares its teeth with huge traffic densities and congestion. This takes some getting used to, especially if the traveller is driving a hire car, on the "wrong" side of the road and in a strange country.

1) Richborough, East Kent coast, just south of Ramsgate.
2) Colchester, Essex. Colchester is on the A12, near to but not on the coast.
3) St Albans, Herts. St Albans is about 30 miles north of London. The old city and cathedral are worth a visit.
4) Canterbury, Kent. Both the city and the cathedral are historic and well worth the effort. Check opening times of the cathedral: it is a busy religious centre and it is often closed to visitors for religious services.

5) Hadrian's Wall, Northumberland. The wall stretches from coast to coast, loosely from Newcastle to Carlisle. There is so much to be seen in the area, the visitor might find it necessary to allow three or four days at least.

6) London Wall to the north of the city of London. Sections of the Roman city wall still survive.

7) Gravesend, North Kent, on the River Thames.

8) R. Camel, North Cornwall.

9) Glastonbury, Somerset. Near Bridgwater. Not far from the famous Cheddar Gorges. The town is interesting and is full of interesting people.

10) Wearmouth. A suburb of Sunderland, County Durham. At the mouth of the River Wear. Not much to recommend it.

11) Bath, Somerset. Famous for its Roman baths. Its name in Roman times was Aquae Sulis. Bannerdown Hill, in the north of Bath, is said to be the Mons Badonicus mentioned in reports of King Arthur's great battle.

12) Fosse Way from Bath to Lincoln.

13) Tamworth, Staffordshire plus Offa's Dyke. Offa's Dyke is still identifiable and can be walked as a whole (it is 189 miles in length) or in sections. For much of its length, it still marks the boundary between England and Wales.

14) York. County city of Yorkshire. Called Eboracum by the Romans, Eorforwic by the Saxons and Yorvik by the Vikings. There is much Roman and ecclesiastical history in this rather pleasing city.

15) Corfe, Dorset. Corfe Castle was badly damaged during the English Civil War but large parts of it are intact and can be explored. Between Wareham and Swanage.

16) Northumbria used to mean the entire area north of the Humber. It is now taken to mean the area between Hadrian's Wall (between Newcastle and Carlisle) and the Scottish border. It includes a thinly populated rural area and a national park. Its best known places are Holy Island, Hadrian's Wall and Alnwick Castle.

17) Stamford Bridge, Nottingham.

18) Battle Abbey, near Hastings, West Sussex. Not difficult to reach from London, the Abbey and battle site are well equipped for visitors.

19) Domesday Book. Held at the National Archive, Kew, Richmond, Surrey.

20) The New Forest is the area of woodland and heath land to the west of Southampton Water.

21) Anjou, France. Area surrounding Angers on the R. Loire, France.

22) Runnymede, near Old Windsor. Close to junction 13, M25. Windsor and Eton College can be included with the one trip.

23) Oxford, Oxfordshire. West of London. Colleges etc are open for visitors in the summer, when the students are "down". Oxford is also a good base from which to explore the Cotswolds.

24) Battle of Lewes, Near Brighton, East Sussex.

25) Orkney and Shetland. Orkney and Shetland are off the north coast of Scotland and regard themselves as separate, emphasising their Scandinavian heritage. Shetland is nearer to Bergen in Norway than it is to Edinburgh or London.

26) Snowdonia, North Wales. Apart from abandoned slate mines and quarries, there is not much of historical value, though the area is worth visiting for its own sake.

27) Falkirk, Scotland.

28) Smithfield, London. This is the original Smithfield, in Central London. Be aware that the central markets of London have been moved to more suitable sites and re-named "New ..." but are still referred to by their old names – Smithfield, Covent Garden, Billingsgate etc.

29) Avignon, France.

30) Bosworth. Near Leicester. Bosworth is difficult to get to by any means other than by road. It might be best to travel by train to Hinckley and take a cab from there. Still worth a visit, though.

31) Cadiz, South-western Spain.

32) Plymouth, Devon. Still a major naval base.

33) Calais, France, now the main point of sea-borne entry from Dover.

34) Galway, Eire.

35) La Rochelle, Western France

36) Naseby, Northamptonshire. Between Northampton and Market Harborough, just off the hellish A14 trunk road.

37) Berwick, Northumberland.

38) Newark, Nottinghamshire.

39) Drogheda, Eire, to the north of Dublin

40) Dunbar, on the Midlothian coast, east of Edinburgh.

41) Monument, in the city of London. Lots of Fire of London-related history around here.

42) Chatham, Kent. Chatham is on the Medway, adjacent to and largely merged with Rochester and Gillingham.

43) Killiecrankie, on the A9, north of Perth, Scotland.

44) Glencoe, Loch Leven on the A82, south of Fort William.

45) Londonderry, Ulster.

46) Limerick, Eire, on the west coast. Best known for ribald poetry.

47) Blenheim on R. Danube near Ulm, Germany.

48) Ramillies, Oudenarde, Malplaquet.

49) Blenheim Palace, Woodstock, Oxfordshire, just north of Oxford. Easy to get to, well worth the visit. Allow a whole day for a visit.

50) Darian – now Panama. Famous now only for the Panama Canal.

51) Sherriffmuir, Scotland near Stirling, on Firth of Forth.

52) Prestonpans, to the east of Edinburgh.

53) Culloden Moor, near Inverness.

54) Martello Towers and the Royal Military Canal. The Royal Military Canal still runs along the Kent coast and can be visited easily. A number of Martello towers still exist and can be visited at certain times.

55) HMS Victory, Royal Naval Dockyard, Portsmouth, Hampshire good rail service from London.

56) Island of Elba, between Corsica and Italy's Tuscan coast.

57) Waterloo, on N5 south of Brussels. In the fields between Waterloo and Braine-l'Alleud (Eigenbrakel). The battlefield is just outside the town and tours are freely available. The guides and staff speak English extremely well. There is a Eurostar service from St Pancras to Brussels and the battle site is a few miles to the south.

58) St Helena Island, Atlantic Ocean.

59) Severn Gorge, Coalport, Ironbridge, Shropshire. Probably best by train to Telford, the museum is just to the south of this new town. If you have the time, buy a multi-visit ticket and see everything. Probably take two or three days to see it all.

60) Stockton and Darlington, County Durham. Still an important industrial area.

61) The railway stations are, clockwise from the west: Paddington, Marylebone, Euston, St Pancras, Kings Cross, Liverpool Street and Fenchurch Street. Then, from the east, clockwise, Cannon Street, London Bridge, Blackfriars, Waterloo, Charing Cross and Victoria.

62) (Adolf Hitler, born 20th April 1888 at Braunau am Inn, Austria, where his father was posted as a customs inspector. His family originated from the Waldviertal to the north of Linz. He served in the Bavarian Army during WW1 and emerged from the war a much decorated war veteran. He remained an Austrian subject until 1938, when, following Anschluss – the merger of Austria with Germany – all Austrian citizens became citizens of the German Reich.

OTHER PLACES

South East

Bodiam Castle Not far from Battle. Classic stone castle, probably the best surviving. Everything there, including a moat inhabited by the most enormous fish.

Cinque Ports Dover, Hastings, Hythe, Romney, Sandwich. This whole area of Kent is stuffed with history. If time permits, you could also take in the Royal Military Canal and some Martello Towers – and Battle Abbey is close by.

South West This part of Britain is long and narrow but apart from Stonehenge, there is Avebury Stone Circle, Tregeare Rounds, Tintagel, Corfe Castle and the cathedrals at Salisbury and Winchester.

Eastern England Main places are Cambridge and Ely, as well as Constable Country, just north of Ipswich, where it is possible to take in the views in Constable's paintings, which are pretty much unchanged. For example, at Flatford Mill, the house (then belonging to William Lott) shown in The Haywain, is still there. In the north, there is Walsingham Abbey, a major religious centre.

Midlands Apart from Bosworth and the Ironbridge Gorge, there are a number of towns worth a visit, in particular, Warwick, Ludlow and Shrewsbury.

Bibury: mediaeval village and beauty spot, still inhabited, on the B4425 road between Burford and Cirencester. The famous Arlington Row cottages, much photographed, are 600 years old and still lived in. The River Coln – a trout stream runs through it. This would probably be part of a longer trip to the Cotswolds.

Roman villas are to be seen at Long Hanborough near Witney, Oxfordshire and at Chedworth, near Northleach, Gloucestershire.

North West Mostly, this is an industrial area but further north is the Lake District. Not primarily an historic area, but fame was brought to the area by a group of poets, notably William Wordsworth, Dorothy Wordsworth and Samuel Taylor Coleridge. There are museums and other tourist attractions dedicated to their work. It is an attractive area in its own right.

Scotland Scotland is a very large area with many historic attractions but they are widely spread and might be better treated as a separate entity. You can easily spend three weeks seeing the most important sights.

BRITISH HISTORY IN BRIEF

Orkney and Shetland have stone circles and other pre-historic sites, as well as brochs and burial barrows. If you have the use of a car, Orkney can be reached by the ferries from Scrabster and Gills Bay. Shetland is more difficult and involves an overnight ferry from Aberdeen to Lerwick.

Kings and Queens of England and Their Dates

The House of Mercia

(754-794)   Offa, King of Mercia and ruler of all the Britons.

The House of Wessex

802-839	Egbert
839-855	Aethelwulf
855-860	Aethelbald
860-866	Aethelbert
866-871	Aethelred
871-899	Alfred, *the Great*
899-925	Edward, *the Elder*
925-940	Athelstan
940-946	Edmund, *the Magnificent*
946-955	Eadred
955-959	Eadwig (Eadwy), *All-Fair*
959-975	Edgar, *the Peaceable*
975-978	Edward, *the Martyr*
978-1016	Aethelread, *the Unready*
1016	Edmund, *Ironside*

The Danish line
1014	Svein, *Forkbeard*
1016-1035	Knut (Canute) *the Great*
1035-1040	Harald, *Harefoot*
1040-1042	Hardicanute

House of Wessex, restored
1042-1066	Edward, *the Confessor*
1066	Harold 2nd

The Norman line
1066-1087	Willliam, *the Conqueror*
1087-1100	William 2nd, *Rufus*
1100-1135	Henry 1st *Beauclerc*
1135-1141	Stephen
1141	*Empress* Matilda
1141-1154	Stephen, restored

The Plantagenet, Angevin line
1154-1189	Henry 2nd, *Curtmantle*
1189-1199	Richard, *the Lionheart*
1199 -1216	John, *Lackland*
1216-1272	Henry 3rd
1272-1307	Edward 1st, *Longshanks*
1307-1327	Edward 2nd
1327 -1377	Edward 3rd
1377 – 1399	Richard 2nd

The Plantagenet Lancastrian line
1399-1413	Henry 4th, *Bolingbroke*
1413-1422	Henry 5th
1422-1461	Henry 6th
1470-1471	Henry 6th

The Plantagenet, House of York line

1461-1470	Edward 4th
1471-1483	Edward 4th
1483	Edward 5th
1483-1485	Richard 3rd, *Crookback*

The House of Tudor

1485-1509	Henry 7th
1509-1547	Henry 8th
1547-1543	Edward 6th
1553	Lady Jane Grey
1553-1558	Mary 1st, *Tudor*
1558-1603	Elizabeth 1st

The House of Stuart

1603-1625	James 1st & 6th (of Scotland)
1625-1649	Charles 1st

The Commonwealth

1649-1658	Oliver Cromwell, *Lord Protector*
1658-1659	Richard Cromwell

The Stuarts, restored

1660-1685	Charles 2nd
1685-1688	James 2nd

The House of Orange & Stuart

1689-1702	William 3rd, Mary 2nd
1702-1714	Anne

The House of Brunswick (Hanover)

1714-1727	George 1st
1727-1760	George 2nd

1760-1820	George 3rd
1820-1830	George 4th
1830-1837	William 3rd
1837-1901	Victoria

House of Saxe-Coburg-Gotha

| 1901-1910 | Edward 7th |

House of Windsor

1910-1936	George 5th
1936	Edward 8th (abdicated)
1936-1952	George 6th
1952-present	Elizabeth 2nd

Kings of Scotland

? – 1093	Malcolm 3rd
? – 1124	Alexander 1st
1084-1153	David 1st
1143-1214	William
1198 -1249	Alexander 2nd
1249 -1285	Alexander 3rd
1274 -1328	Robert 1st
1249 -1315	John de Balliol
1316-1390	Robert 2nd
1324 -1371	David 2nd
1394 -1437	James 1st
1512-1542	James 5th

Shakespeare's Plays and Dates

The dates given here are those of the first performance. There is no record of them having been written down at the time. Some of them were committed to paper as much as thirty years after the first performance, suggesting that some development of the play took place over the intervening years. Shakespeare had to be careful politically, certainly while Queen Elizabeth 1 reigned and probably after James Stuart came to the throne in 1603, so it is likely that any changes would have taken into account changes in the political atmosphere.

PLAY	FIRST PERFORMED
Henry VI, part 2	1591
Henry VI part 3	1591
Henry VI part 1	1591
Richard III	1593
Comedy of Errors	1593
Titus Andronicus	1594
Taming of the Shrew	1594
Two Gentlemen of Verona	1595
Love's Labours Lost	1595
Romeo and Juliet	1595
Richard II	1596
Midsummer Night's Dream	1596

King John	1597
Merchant of Venice	1597
Henry IV, part 1	1598
Henry IV, part 2	1598
Much Ado About Nothing	1599
Henry V	1599
Julius Caesar	1600
Hamlet	1601
Merry Wives of Windsor	1601
Troilus and Cressida	1602
All's Well That Ends Well	1603
Measure for Measure	1604
Othello	1605
King Lear	1605
Macbeth	1606
Antony and Cleopatra	1607
Coriolanus	1607
Timon of Athens	1608
Pericles	1608
Cymbeline	1609
The Winter's Tale	1610
The Tempest	1611
Henry VIII	1612

Pronunciation of Place Names

Alcester	Alster
Aldburgh	Aldbruh
Alnwick	Annick
Berwick	Berrick
BettwysyCoed	Bettiss–e–Coyd
Bicester	Bister
Caernarfon	Curnarven
Cirencester	Sirensester
Dolgellau	Dolgethli
Edinburgh	Edinbruh
Folkstone	Fokestun
Gloucester	Gloster
Garboldisham	Garbisham
Heysham	Heesham
Hunstanton	Hunston
Keswick	Kezick
Leicester	Lester
Llanelli	Tlanethli
Llangollen	Tlangothlan
Mousehole	Moozel
Stiffkey	Stukey
Woolfardisworthy	Woolsery
Worcester	Wooster
Wymondham	Windham

The Origins of British Place Names

The names of villages, towns and cities in Britain originate from the names given by earlier settlers. In particular, in England, names have been given to settlements and subsequently been changed or modified by subsequent settlers or conquerors. For example, the City of York has been known by several names. The Romans called it Eboracum but this may not be an original name: it may well be a "Latinised" name developed from a name given by the ancient Britons. After the Romans left, the Angles took over and called it Eorforwic. Subsequently, the Vikings took over the settlement and called it Jorvik. The English called the place York, although it should be remembered that the Archbishop of York still signs himself Ebor.

Here is an indication of the origin of some of the parts of names which give some clue to the origin of the settlement. It should be remembered that, as the population expanded, so did towns and cities. In the process, surrounding villages were swallowed up and the names of those villages survive as indistinct districts. The abbreviation S means the term is used as a suffix and the end of a name; P means a prefix, normally at the beginning of a name.

157

NAME	P/S	ORIGIN	TRANSLATION
Aber	P	Celtic	River mouth
Borough, Burgh, Bury	S	Saxon	Fortified place
By	S	Norse	Farm, village
Caer	P	Celtic	Fortress
Caster, Chester	S	Roman	City, Camp
Don, Down, dun	S	Saxon	Hill
Ford	S	Saxon	River crossing
Hurst	P/S	Saxon	Hillock, copse
Ing	S	Saxon	People
Ingham	S	Saxon	Homestead of (name)'s people
Ley, Leigh, Ly	S	Saxon	Wood
Shaw	S	Saxon	Small wood
Stow	P/S	Saxon	Holy place
Thwaite	S	Norse	Meadow, paddock
Toft	S	Norse	Homestead
Ton	S	Saxon	Town
Tre	P	Celtic	Farmstead
Wick	S	Norse/Saxon	Bay (Norse) Farm (Saxon)
Wold	P/S	Saxon	Hill
Worth	S	Saxon	Enclosure

Further Reading

Anglo-Saxon Chronicles: Traditional

Britain Begins: Sir Barry Cunliffe, Oxford University Press 2013

On the ruination of Britain: Gildas the Wise AD 516

The Ecclesiastical History of the English People: The Venerable Bede AD 731.
Oxford World's Classics

Anglo Saxon England: Sir Frank Stenton 1971. Oxford University Press

A History of Christianity: Diarmuid MacCulloch 2009 Penguin Books

A History of Roman Britain: Peter Salway 1993 Oxford University Press

Roman Britain and the English Settlements: 1968 R.G.Collingwood &
J.L.N.Myers

The Crusades: Thomas Asbridge 2010 Simon & Schuster

Boudica's Last Stand: John Waite, History Press

Book of the Somme: Malcolm Brown Imperial War Museum 1996

The Road to Verdun: Ian Ousby Jonathan Cape 2002

First World War: John Keegan Pimlico 1999

Forgotten Victory: Gary Sheffield 2001 Headline

Population of Britain Throughout History

Before the first census of 1801, figures given for population in Britain are estimates. Those estimates suggest that, just after the last Ice Age, the population numbered a few thousand and remained fairly constant until the Roman era, when it is thought that the population might have risen to as many as five million. It may be that the constant conflicts of the next six hundred years, together with the food shortages that accompanied them, probably reduced the population considerably. We can be reasonably certain that by the year 1000 AD, the population was no more than about 1.5-2 million. Over the next three centuries, that figure doubled, but the Black Death in the mid-fourteenth century wiped out all those gains, bringing the population back to what it was at the time of the Norman invasion. A recovery over the next century and a half saw the population rise to probably six million and, by the year 1600 AD, reach eight million.

There then began a period of very rapid growth of population. By 1700AD the country was home to just under 10 million people and by 1800 AD, seventeen million. At the beginning of the 20th Century, we had forty-one million. Population growth slowed during the first half of the 20th Century, almost certainly the effect of the two world wars. In 1946, for example, the population is recorded at forty-eight million.

Since the end of the war, despite a few surges in the birth rate, the population of the native population has grown only slowly and in recent decades its birth rate has fallen below replacement rate. However, the population has grown nevertheless as a result of immigration and the relatively high birth rates among the new migrants. In 2014, the population of Britain stood at sixty-four million.

Index